DONATION

MORE HEARTWARMING TALES

OF HOLIDAY JOY

*

Christmas

in

My Heart

A SECOND TREASURY

*

Compiled and Edited by

JOE WHEELER

Guideposts.
CARMEL, NEW YORK 10512

www.guidepostsbooks.com

The Thirty-six Days of Christmas

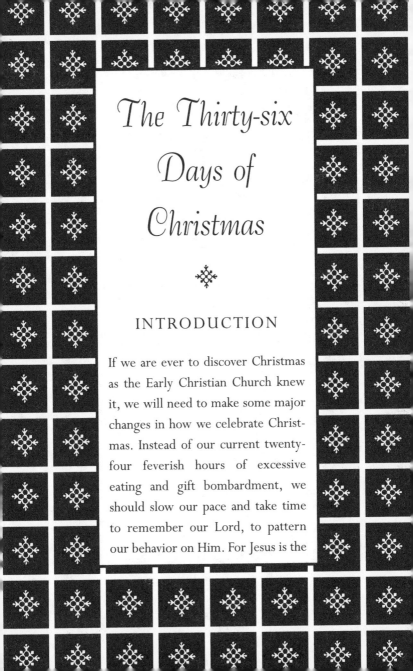

INTRODUCTION

If we are ever to discover Christmas as the Early Christian Church knew it, we will need to make some major changes in how we celebrate Christmas. Instead of our current twenty-four feverish hours of excessive eating and gift bombardment, we should slow our pace and take time to remember our Lord, to pattern our behavior on Him. For Jesus is the greatest prototype of selfless giving and service for others that the world has ever known.

Most merchants won't be happy with us for making such a change, for today Christmas has degenerated into merely another seasonal sale. We become preoccupied with things and get tired out by the countdown to Christmas.

We will begin the year, as did the Early Church, with the season of the Advent. Around the first of December, we will turn off the television set and leave it off for thirty-six days. In the place of television, we will set up as the focal center of our lives a manger scene, or crèche. We will post an Advent calendar and plan family activities that reflect on the spiritual dimensions of the season. Instead of watching beer commercials that shamelessly trade on Christ's birth, we will take the family to attend sacred concerts, oratorios, and pageants. All the jolly commercial Santa Clauses will be traded in for the self-giving spirit of St. Nicholas, and we will visit and serve those less fortunate than ourselves. Each evening during the twenty-four days of Advent, we will gather around the fireside, share Christmas stories, sing and perform Christian music, and fellowship with our extended family.

It will be a time to cut the power to the glaring lights and substitute the serenity of fireside, candles, and kerosene lamps. We will craft gifts rather than merely buying them in a shopping mall.

When Christmas Eve arrives, and the bells of midnight are followed by Christmas morning, there will yet remain the twelve days of Christmas, culminating with the Day of the Magi (also known as the Epiphany) on January 6.

As was true with the Early Church, the emphasis during the Advent will be on Christ's birth in the flesh, in Bethlehem, the miracle of incarnation. But also important are the concluding twelve days. To early Christians, these represented the days that led up to Christ's second birth, His baptism in the Jordan River. It was then that the Holy Spirit descended upon Him as a dove and, with the Father, testified publicly that the divine circle of three was united for the awesome task ahead.

In much of the Christian world today, on each of these twelve days, gifts are given. Often children are given one gift a day, and in turn may themselves give gifts—much like the Jewish Hanukkah celebration. On January 6, more than one gift is given.

For us and our families, these days can be joyous times. Note this serendipity: New Year's Day divides the twelve days in half. On this day, the family can take time to give thanks, take stock of the past year and the many blessings it has brought, make New Year's resolutions, and look forward to the year to come.

On the seventh day of January, we will tenderly pack up the nativity figures and make plans for the next season.

If we are to be successful in reclaiming Christmas from our materialistic culture, we shall have to fill the time once wasted on mindless entertainment with something more profitable, something more in tune with the divine. We will need to develop new traditions.

LAS POSADAS

Perhaps one of the reasons I still have a childlike love for Christmas is that I was lucky enough to be brought up in two distinctly different cultures: North America and Latin America. I was barely nine when our family left California for Panama (and then Costa Rica, Guatemala, the Dominican Republic, and Mexico). In our home, we waited out that interminable period of time between November 30 and Christmas Eve. But finally it would come. Mother would read us Christmas stories, we would think about the birth of our Lord, we would open the gifts under the pine Christmas tree—and within hours it would all be over for another year.

Not so with my Latino playmates. For them, the season began during the last days of November, and the enthusiasm and excitement built steadily. In each home would be a crèche, and colorful flowers filled the houses. Since I was clearly jealous of my friends, my folks gladly let me purchase nativity figures and arrange my own crèche each year.

Children are loved everywhere, but nowhere, it seems to me, more than south of the border. (I'll never forget the first time I awoke at five o'clock on the morning of my birthday to the haunting chords of "Las Mañanitas." My adult friends loved me enough to crawl out of bed in the dead of night, dress, gather with other friends and relatives, tune the guitar, walk to our house, position themselves outside my window, and sing to me. *Me*—just a child!)

If you really want to celebrate a multidimensional Christmas, go to Mexico. It is a proud country, rich in traditions, and a place we can learn much from. The season is one children revel in, for it is a joyous time.

The Christmas season actually starts with the twelfth of December, the Virgin of Guadalupe Day; other than Christmas itself, no day means more to Mexicans than this. It is a national holiday, a day in which to make pilgrimages.

But to me, one of the loveliest Christmas traditions I know is *Las Posadas,* beginning four days later on December

16. Prior to that day, however, most homes will have been decorated with paper lanterns, Spanish moss, white lilies, and evergreens. And the focal center of the Christmas season will be an altar, a nativity scene, or crèche.

Starting near the first of December, children's thoughts center increasingly on the coming nine nights. Who will get to be the Virgin Mary? Who will get to be Joseph? Who will get to be with the hard-hearted innkeeper when Mary and Joseph seek *posada* (a place to rest for the night), and who will at last get to welcome them in? Every time children pass their crèche, their thoughts turn to that dramatic reenactment only days away.

Finally, on the night of December 16, nine families choreograph the festivities. The starring roles are assigned to children. At certain homes, as the guests and extended family arrive, they are arbitrarily separated into two groups: the cruel innkeepers and the holy pilgrims. Each pilgrim is handed a lighted candle, and a procession is formed, with an angel leading the way, followed by Mary, Joseph, and the pilgrims.

No one who has ever seen *Las Posadas* can possibly forget how moving it is. Once it begins, all else in the life of the town seems to stop while the two-thousand-year-old drama is once again played out.

The long journey from Nazareth to Bethlehem is represented by two children. Carrying his staff, Joseph leads a donkey. On the donkey's plump back is the most precious thing in the universe: little Mary, who, we "know," carries within her the Savior of the world. Friends and relatives surround the pair as they make their way down the street. These friends also are attired in costumes of the time. The mood is set by candlelight and sacred music. Joseph and Mary and their attendants stop at nine houses. At each door, Joseph pleads for *posada;* at each door, he is unceremoniously turned away. Except at the ninth house—the door is opened wide, the procession comes in, and all sing their thanks.

For nine consecutive nights, the pageant is repeated. But each time it is different, for on each night, *posada* is offered at a different home.

Armando Gonzales, a poet and Mexican folklore specialist in Rosarito, tells me that the institution of *Las Posadas* actually came to Mexico from Spain, but in a form that was not nearly as developed as it is today. Furthermore, as it is conducted today, there is a great deal of flexibility in terms of how it is done. For instance, since *Las Posadas* symbolizes the nine-day journey from Nazareth to Bethlehem, *Las Posadas* can be done between towns—in fact, that would be the most historically accurate way—with the couple asking for *posada* each night in a different town. If it is a small town, everyone participates in just the one reenactment. Mr. Gonzales recalls that, in larger towns and cities, there are likely to be a number of *posadas* all going on at once. He remembers the fun of moving from *posada* to *posada,* and catching the magic and uniqueness of each one—and, not incidentally, reveling in all the good food and hot drinks at those ninth houses!

Mr. Gonzales remembers one *posada* with great vividness. It was in the mountains, overpowering because of its unexpectedness: suddenly, from all directions, coming down the mountains came a glow—resulting from *many* candles—and it turned out to be a gathering of *posada* participants from the entire region!

Mr. Gonzales noted that there is much memorization involved, for the ritual of what is said and what is sung is perhaps the most formalized aspect of the entire pageant. At each house, they sing the various parts of "The Litany of Loretto." Finally Joseph comes to a door and mournfully begs *entrada* (entrance):

> In heaven's name, I beg for shelter.
> My wife tonight can go no farther.

Those inside, with the hard-hearted innkeeper (usually all male), angrily reply:

No inn is this. Begone from hence.
Ye may be thieves.

At the ninth house, *los santos pelegrinos* (the holy pilgrims) are joyously welcomed in; the pilgrims go to an improvised altar decorated with toys of all sorts. The party kneels and says prayers.

The last night *(La Noche Buena)* is the most lavish of all, and *posada* is usually at the home of someone affluent enough to entertain a lot of guests. In this home, the altar is beautifully decorated with tinsel and flowers, and the Infant Jesus is found in a moss-lined crib. The whole party sings many more songs—almost a book of them—and that is followed with food, sweets, liquors, and dancing until it is time to go to the cathedral for midnight mass.

Also each evening, blindfolded children take turns swinging at *piñatas*—then, when one eventually smashes it, there is a wild scramble for the shower of fruits, gifts, and candy.

I asked Mr. Gonzales how late the children were kept up—and he laughed. "In Mexico," he said, "during this period of the year, nobody worries much about bedtime. Even after midnight, there is likely to be many hours of eating, laughing, singing, dancing, and celebration—and the children are part of it. . . . As a child, I loved it!"

"What about the rest of the season?" I asked. Mr. Gonzales responded, "Well, there's lots more to look forward to: on Christmas Day, each child usually receives a very special gift or two, something long desired. But the Santa Claus-induced glut of presents typical north of the border is strongly resisted; instead, children look forward to *El Día de los Sántos Reyes* on January 6; on the evening of the fifth, each child puts out his/her shoes, and, the next morning, there are all their presents—left by the Wise Men!

"But before that there is *Día de los Inocentes* [the Day of the Innocents] on December 28."

"And what is that day all about?" I asked.

"Don't you remember—Herod's slaughter of the Bethlehem babies?"

"Oh, yes! But . . . what kind of a holiday would *that* be? Sounds kind of bloody."

"Not so! In fact, it is a day like your April Fools' Day in the United States." And then he chuckled. "If anyone is foolish enough to forget what day it is, he's in *big* trouble, for nothing one says or does on that day can be taken seriously. For instance, if I ask you if I can borrow twenty dollars—and you are gullible enough to lend it to me . . . you'll never see it again. It's *gone!*"

"Then we have New Year's—a big celebration everywhere. But another very special holiday is January 5, the day before Epiphany. That's a holiday Maximilian and Carlotta brought over to us from Europe. On this day and eve, we eat *bolillas* . . ."

"What are they?"

"Well, sort of a European baguette [French roll]. . . . But the most fun comes from the *Rosca de Reyes*."

"Huh? What are they?"

"Oh, sort of like a gigantic sugared doughnut—we can thank our good Emperor and Empress for introducing them."

"Doesn't sound that funny to *me*."

"Oh! Sorry—forgot to tell you. Inside certain *Rosca de Reyes* are little plastic babies baked in the dough—and whoever chomps down on one is in trouble!"

"How's that?"

"Well, he or she has to invite to a special party on *Día de la Candelaria* [Candlemas], February 2, *every last person* who is in the room when he or she bites down on the plastic baby! . . . It can get expensive. *Very* expensive!" And Mr. Gonzales chuckled reminiscently. I sensed that he had been one of those "unlucky" ones.

He said a lot more. . . . And I have thought a lot about what he said. What came across to me was this: the Mexican people derive great joy out of their holidays, which are far more of a family time than our Christmas tends to be. Although they combine the spiritual and the secular just as we do, they never let their families forget that the spiritual dimension is paramount.

And I thought back to the last *posada* I experienced—it was in Taxco on *La Noche Buena* (Christmas Eve). Even now, a quarter of a century later, I can still envision that moment when the procession was welcomed into the inn where my wife and I were staying: the sweet, high sounds of the children's voices as they sang, and above all, the boy who, for the moment, *was* Joseph, and the girl who *was* Mary.

When I compare that feeling of reverence and awe to Christmas in America, I could cry. On that holiest of nights, *La Noche Buena,* all over America children are ripping paper off gaily wrapped packages, scanning the contents, and feverishly grabbing the next. But in much of the Christian world, children are preparing to go with their parents to the cathedral, the church, or chapel, there to see the nativity scene; there to hear the Christmas music, the mighty organ, and the midnight bells welcoming the birth of the Christ child.

The next morning is a joyful one for those children, but not because of avalanches of presents, although there may be a few. There is no Santa Claus, for, after all, they are celebrating the Lord's birth. There are yet twelve more wonderful Christmas days before that most anticipated day, January 6.

I can still remember how excited my friends next door were as they eagerly waited for the religious procession of the Three Kings, and the gifts the kings would leave for them during the night. The Magi. Not Santa Claus.

It's not that I am against Santa Claus, for he represents another special part of my Christmas memories: I can hear, in my memory, my red-and-white-suited Santa of a father playing Christmas carols on his harmonica as he draws near the front door every year. But I am saddened that the life and ministry of a wonderful and generous Christian gentleman, St. Nicholas, has been perverted to the pandering of seasonal merchandise to avaricious children, vigorously encouraged to greed beyond belief by the advertising media and those who buy their services.

Is it strange that I long for the thirty-six days of Christmas as they are enjoyed south of the border?

THE SECOND COLLECTION

It has been an exciting year. As many of you know, *Christmas in My Heart* was born in 1992 (Review & Herald), and took awhile before it really began to move. But that was in paperback. In 1996 Doubleday and I decided to repackage the series: rearrange, reillustrate, move from paperback to hardback, from horizontal to vertical format, from large to small size, and from the comparatively small Christian book market to the general market.

With the success of Doubleday's *Christmas in My Heart,* everyone urged us to get out another collection for Christmas 1997. But most significant of all, so many noted that the two most meaningful things about the series were: (1) that the stories hit on an emotional gut level, and (2) that the stories were Christ-centered rather than Santa Claus-centered. And a number of you have responded to our plea, and are sending us your personal favorite stories. We thank you!

I will now put myself out on a limb: it is my sincere conviction that never, since I first began putting together story collections, have I put together a more powerful collection of stories than these. But that is only *my* conviction—the real proof will be in *your* responses!

❖

CODA

I look forward to hearing from you—and please do keep the stories, responses, and suggestions coming. And not just Christmas stories: I'm putting together collections centered around other genres as well. You may contact me at the following address:

Joe Wheeler, Ph.D.
c/o Doubleday Religion Department
1540 Broadway
New York, New York 10036

David's Star

of Bethlehem

❄

CHRISTINE WHITING
PARMENTER

*I was still young when I first remember my
mother reciting this particular story. It's a
story I defy any red-blooded human to listen to—or read—dry-eyed. All the
tragedy of cruelty, loss, inhumanity, and
death are here, just as are the sublimity of
love, caring, restoration, and happiness.
Through the years it has become a Christmas season classic.*

Christine   Whiting   Parmenter

(1877–1953) wrote prolifically in popular and religious journals early in the twentieth century. Besides stories, she also wrote a number of full-length books. Today, few people have heard of her, but she deserves to be brought back. I would guess that "David's Star of Bethlehem," to story aficionados, is one of the ten most beloved Christmas stories ever written.

Scott Carson reached home in a bad humor. Nancy, slipping a telltale bit of red ribbon into her workbasket, realized this as soon as he came in.

It was the twenty-first of December, and a white Christmas was promised. Snow had been falling for hours, and in most of the houses wreaths were already in the windows. It was what one calls "a Christmasy-feeling day," yet, save for that red ribbon in Nancy's basket, there was no sign in the Carson home of the approaching festival.

Scott said, kissing her absentmindedly and slumping into a big chair, "This snow is the very limit. If the wind starts blowing, there'll be a fierce time with the traffic. My train was twenty minutes late as it was, and—there's the bell. Who can it be at this hour? I want my dinner."

"I'll go to the door," said Nancy hurriedly as he started up. "Selma's putting dinner on the table now."

Relaxing into his chair, Scott heard her open the front door, say something about the storm, and, after a moment, wish someone a merry Christmas.

A merry Christmas! He wondered that she could say it so calmly. Three years ago on Christmas morning, they had lost their boy—swiftly—terribly—without warning. Meningitis, the doctor said. Only a few hours before, the child had seemed a healthy, happy youngster, helping them trim the tree; hoping, with a twinkle in the brown eyes so like his mother's, that Santa Claus would remember the fact that he wanted skis! He had gone happily to bed after Nancy had read them "The Night Before Christmas," a custom of early childhood's days that the eleven-year-old lad still clung to. Later his mother remembered, with a pang, that when she kissed him good night he had said his head felt "kind of funny." But she had left him lightheartedly enough and gone down to help Scott fill the stockings. Santa had not forgotten the skis; but Jimmy never saw them.

Three years—and the memory still hurt so much that the very thought of Christmas was agony to Scott Carson. Jimmy had slipped away just as the carolers stopped inno-cently beneath his window, their voices rising clear and penetrating on the dawn-sweet air:

" 'Silent night, holy night . . .' "

Scott rose suddenly. He *must* not live over that time again. "Who was it?" he asked gruffly as Nancy joined him, and understanding the gruffness she answered tactfully, "Only the expressman."

"What'd he bring?"

"Just a—a package."

"One naturally supposes that," replied her husband with a touch of sarcasm. Then, suspicion gripping him, he burst out, "Look here! If you've been getting a Christmas gift for me, I—I won't have it. I told you I wanted to forget Christmas. I—"

"I know, dear," she broke in hastily. "The package was only from Aunt Mary."

"Didn't you tell her we weren't keeping Christmas?" he demanded irritably.

"Yes, Scott; but—but you know Aunt Mary! Come now, dinner's on and I think it's a good one. You'll feel better after you eat."

But Scott found it unaccountably hard to eat; and later, when Nancy was reading aloud in an effort to soothe him, he could not follow. She had chosen something humorous and diverting; but in the midst of a paragraph he spoke, and she knew that he had not been listening.

❖

"Nancy," he said, "is there anyplace—anyplace on God's earth where we can get away from Christmas?"

She looked up, answering with sweet gentleness, "It would be a hard place to find, Scott."

He faced her suddenly. "I feel as if I couldn't stand it—the trees—the carols—the merrymaking, you know. Oh, if I could only sleep this week away! But . . . I've been thinking . . . Would—would you consider for one moment going up to camp with me for a day or two? I'd go alone, but—"

"Alone!" she echoed. "Up there in the wilderness at Christmastime? Do you think I'd let you?"

"But it would be hard for you, dear, cold and uncomfortable. I'm a brute to ask it, and yet—"

Nancy was thinking rapidly. They could not escape Christmas, of course. No change of locality could make them forget the anniversary of the day that Jimmy went away. But she was worried about Scott, and the change of scene might help him over the difficult hours ahead. The camp, situated on the mountain a mile from any neighbors, would at least be isolated. There was plenty of bedding, and a big fireplace. It was worth trying.

She said, cheerfully, "I'll go with you, dear. Perhaps the change will make things easier for both of us."

This was Tuesday, and on Thursday afternoon they stepped off the northbound train and stood on the platform watching it vanish into the mountains. The day was crisp and cold! "Two above," the stationmaster told them as they went into the box of a station and moved instinctively toward the red-hot "airtight" stove which gave forth grateful warmth.

"I sent a telegram yesterday to Clem Hawkins, over on the mountain road," said Scott. "I know you don't deliver a message so far off; but I took a chance. Do you know if he got it?"

"Yep. Clem don't have a phone, but the boy came down for some groceries and I sent it up. If I was you, though, I'd stay to the central house. Seems as if it would be more cheerful—Christmastime."

"I guess we'll be comfortable enough if Hawkins airs out, and lights a fire," replied Scott, his face hardening at this innocent mention of the holiday. "Is there anyone around here who'll take us up? I'll pay well for it, of course."

"Ira Morse'll go; but you'll have to walk from

Hawkinses'. The road ain't dug out beyond . . . There's Ira now. You wait, an' I'll holler to him. Hey, Ira!" he called, going to the door. "Will you carry these folks up to Hawkinses'? They'll pay for it."

"Iry," a ruddy-faced young farmer, obligingly appeared, his gray workhorse hitched to a one-seated sleigh of ancient and uncomfortable design.

"Have to sit three on a seat," he explained cheerfully, "but we'll be all the warmer for it. Tuck the buffalo robe 'round the lady's feet, mister, and you and me'll use the horse blanket. Want to stop to the store for provisions?"

"Yes, I brought some canned stuff, but we'll need other things," said Nancy. "I've made a list."

"Well, you got good courage," grinned the station-master. "I hope you don't get froze to death up in the woods. Merry Christmas to you, anyhow."

"The same to you!" responded Nancy, smiling, and noted with a stab of pain that her husband's sensitive lips were trembling.

Under Ira's cheerful conversation, however, Scott relaxed. They talked of crops, the neighbors, and local politics—safe subjects all; but as they passed the district school, where a half dozen sleighs or flivers were parked, the man explained: "Folks decoratin' the school for the

23

doin's tomorrow afternoon. Christmas tree for the kids, and pieces spoke, and singin'. We got a real live school-ma'am this year, believe me!"

They had reached the road that wound up the mountain toward the Hawkins farm, and as they plodded on, a sudden wind arose that cut their faces. Snow creaked under the runners, and as the sun sank behind the mountain Nancy shivered, not so much with cold as with a sense of loneliness and isolation. It was Scott's voice that roused her:

"Should have brought snowshoes. I didn't realize that we couldn't be carried all the way."

"Guess you'll get there all right," said Ira. "Snow's packed hard as a drumhead, and it ain't likely to thaw yet a while. Here you are," as he drew up before the weather-beaten, unpainted farmhouse. "You better step inside a minute and warm up."

A shrewish-looking woman was already at the door, opening it but a crack, in order to keep out fresh air and cold.

"I think," said Nancy with a glance at the deepening shadows, "that we'd better keep right on. I wonder if there's anybody here who'd help carry our bags and provisions."

"There ain't," answered the woman, stepping outside

and pulling a faded gray sweater around her shoulders. "Clem's gone to East Conroy with the eggs, and Dave's up to the camp keepin' yer fire going! You can take the sled and carry yer stuff on that. There 'tis, by the gate. Dave'll bring it back when he comes. An' tell him to hurry. Like as not, Clem won't be back in time fer milkin'."

"I thought Dave was goin' to help Teacher decorate the school this afternoon," ventured Ira. He was unloading their things as he spoke, and roping them to the sled.

"So'd he," responded the woman. "But there w'ant no one else to light that fire, was they? Guess it won't hurt him none to work for his livin' like other folks. That new schoolma'am, she thinks o' nothin' but—"

"Oh, look here!" said the young man, straightening up, a belligerent light in his blue eyes. "It's Christmas! Can Dave go back with me if I stop and milk for him? They'll be workin' all evenin'—lots o' fun for a kid like him, and—"

"No, he can't!" snapped the woman. "His head's enough turned now with speakin' pieces and singin' silly songs. You better be gettin' on, folks. I can't stand here talkin' till mornin'."

She slammed the door, while Ira glared after her retreating figure, kicked the gatepost to relieve his feelings, and then grinned sheepishly.

"Some grouch! Why, she didn't even ask you in to get

25

warm! Well, I wouldn't loiter if I was you. And send that kid right back, or he'll get worse'n a tongue-lashin'. Well, goodbye to you, folks. Hope you have a merry Christmas."

The tramp up the mountain passed almost entirely in silence, for it took their united energy to drag the sled up that steep grade against the wind. Scott drew a breath of relief when they beheld the camp, a spiral of smoke rising from its big stone chimney like a welcome promise of warmth.

"Looks good, doesn't it? But it'll be dark before that boy gets home. I wonder how old—"

They stopped simultaneously as a clear, sweet voice sounded from within the cabin:

" 'Silent night, holy night . . .' "

Scott's face went suddenly dead white. He threw out a hand as if to brush something away, but Nancy caught it in hers, pulling it close against her wildly beating heart.

" 'All is calm . . . all is bright.' "

The childish treble came weirdly from within, while Nancy cried, "Scott—dearest, don't let go! It's only the little boy singing the carols he's learned in school. Don't you see? Come! Pull yourself together. We must go in."

Even as she spoke the door swung open, and through blurred vision they beheld the figure of a boy standing on the threshold. He was a slim little boy with an old, oddly wistful face, and big brown eyes under a thatch of yellow hair.

"You the city folks that was comin' up? Here, I'll help carry in your things."

Before either could protest he was down on his knees in the snow, untying Ira's knots with skillful fingers. He would have lifted the heavy suitcase himself had not Scott, jerked back to the present by the boy's action, interfered.

"I'll carry that in." His voice sounded queer and shaky. "You take the basket. We're late, I'm afraid. You'd better hurry home before it gets too dark. Your mother said—"

"I don't mind the dark," said the boy quietly as they went within. "I'll coast most o' the way down, anyhow. Guess you heard me singin' when you come along." He smiled a shy, embarrassed smile as he explained: "It was a good chance to practice the Christmas carols. They won't let me, 'round home. We're goin' to have a show at the school tomorrow. I'm one o' the three kings—you know—'We Three Kings of Orient Are.' I sing the first verse all by myself," he added with childish pride.

There followed a moment's silence. Nancy was fighting a desire to put her arms around the slim boyish figure, while Scott had turned away, unbuckling the straps of his suitcase with fumbling hands. Then Nancy said, "I'm afraid we've kept you from helping at the school this afternoon. I'm so sorry."

The boy drew a resigned breath that struck her as strangely unchildlike.

"You needn't mind, ma'am. Maybe they wouldn't have let me go anyway; and I've got tomorrow to think about. I—I been reading one o' your books. I like to read."

"What book was it? Would you like to take it home with you for a"—she glanced at Scott, still on his knees by the suitcase, and finished hurriedly—"a Christmas gift?"

"Wouldn't I?" His wistful eyes brightened, then clouded. "Is there a place maybe where I could hide it 'round here? They don't like me to read much to home. They"—a hard look crept into his young eyes—"they burned up a book Teacher gave me a while back. It was *David Copperfield,* and I hadn't got it finished."

There came a crash as Scott, rising suddenly, upset a

chair. The child jumped, and then laughed at himself for being startled.

"Look here, sonny," said Scott huskily, "you must be getting home. Can you bring us some milk tomorrow? I'll find a place to hide your book and tell you about it then. Haven't you got a warmer coat than this?"

He lifted a shabby jacket from the settee and held it out while the boy slipped into it.

"Thanks, mister," he said. "It's hard gettin' it on because it's tore inside. They's only one button," he added as Scott groped for them. "She don't get much time to sew 'em on. I'll bring up the milk tomorrow mornin'. I got to hurry now or I'll get fits! Thanks for the book, ma'am. I'd like *it* better'n anything. Good night."

Standing at the window, Nancy watched him start out in the fast-descending dusk. It hurt her to think of the lonely walk, but she thrust the thought aside and turned to Scott, who had lighted a fire on the hearth and seemed absorbed in the dancing flames.

"That's good!" she said cheerfully. "I'll get things started for supper, and then make the bed. I'm weary enough to turn in early. You might bring me the canned stuff in your suitcase, Scott. A hot soup ought to taste good tonight."

She took an apron from her bag and moved toward the tiny kitchen. Dave evidently knew how to build a fire. The stove lids were almost red, and the kettle was singing. Nancy went about her preparations deftly, tired though she was from the unaccustomed tramp, while Scott opened a can of soup, toasted some bread, and carried their meal on a tray to the settles before the hearth fire. It was all very cozy and "Christmasy," thought Nancy, with the wind blustering outside and the flames leaping up the chimney. But she was strangely quiet. The thought of that lonely little figure trudging off in the gray dusk persisted, despite her efforts to forget. It was Scott who spoke, saying out of a silence, "I wonder how old he is."

"The—the little boy?"

He nodded, and she answered gently, "He seemed no older than—I mean, he seemed very young to be milking cows and doing chores."

Again Scott nodded, and a moment passed before he said, "The work wouldn't hurt him, though, if he were strong enough; but—did you notice, Nancy, he didn't look half-fed? He is an intelligent little chap, though, and his voice— Goodness!" he broke off suddenly. "How can a shrew like that bring such a child into the world? To burn his book!

30

Nancy, I can't understand how things are ordered. Here's that poor boy struggling for development in an unhappy atmosphere—and our Jimmy, who had love, and understanding, and— Tell me, why is it?"

She stretched out a tender hand; but the question remained unanswered, and the meal was finished in silence.

Dave did not come with the milk next morning. They waited till nearly noon, and then tramped off in the snow-clad, pine-scented woods. It was a glorious day, with diamonds sparkling on every fir tree, and they came back refreshed and ravenous for their delayed meal. Scott wiped the dishes, whistling as he worked. It struck his wife that he hadn't whistled like that for months. Later, the last kitchen rites accomplished, she went to the window, where he stood gazing down the trail.

"He won't come now, Scott."

"The kid? It's not three o'clock yet, Nancy."

"But the party begins at four. I suppose everyone for miles around will be there. I wish—" She was about to add that she wished they could have gone too, but something in Scott's face stopped the words. She said instead, "Do you think we'd better go for the milk ourselves?"

"What's the use? They'll all be at the shindig, even that sour-faced woman, I suppose. But somehow—I feel worried about the boy. If he isn't here bright and early in the morning, I'll go down and see what's happened. Looks as if it were clouding up again, doesn't it? Perhaps we'll get snowed in!"

Big, lazy-looking snowflakes were already beginning to drift down. Scott piled more wood on the fire, and stretched out on the settee for a nap. But Nancy was restless. She found herself standing repeatedly at the window, looking at the snow. She was there when at last Scott stirred and wakened. He sat up blinking, and asked, noting the twilight, "How long have I been asleep?"

Nancy laughed, relieved to hear his voice after the long stillness.

"It's after five."

"Good thunder!" He arose, putting an arm across her shoulders. "Poor girl! I haven't been much company on this trip! But I didn't sleep well last night, couldn't get that boy out of my mind. Why, look!" Scott was staring out the window into the growing dusk. "Here he is now. I thought you said—"

He was already at the door, flinging it wide in welcome as he went out to lift the box of milk jars from the sled. It seemed to Nancy, as the child stepped inside, that he looked subtly different—discouraged, she would have said of an older person; and when he raised his eyes she saw the unmistakable sign of recent tears.

"Oh, David!" she exclaimed. "Why aren't you at the party?"

"I didn't go."

The boy seemed curiously to have withdrawn into himself. His answer was like a gentle "none of your business," but Nancy was not without knowledge of boy nature. She thought, *He's hurt—dreadfully. He's afraid to talk for fear he'll cry; but he'll feel better to get it off his mind.* She said, drawing him toward the cheerful hearth fire, "But why not, Dave?"

He swallowed, pulling himself together with a heroic effort.

"I had ter milk. The folks have gone to Conroy to Gramma Hawkins's! I *like* Gramma Hawkins. She told 'em to be sure an' bring me; but there wasn't no one else ter milk, so . . . so . . ."

It was Scott who came to the rescue as David's voice failed suddenly.

"Are you telling us that your people have gone away, for *Christmas,* leaving you home alone?"

The boy nodded, winking back tears as he managed a pathetic smile.

"Oh, I wouldn't ha' minded so much if—if it hadn't been for the doin's at the school. Miss Mary was countin' on me ter sing, and speak a piece. I don't know who they

33

could ha' got to be that wise man." His face hardened in a way not good to see in a little boy, and he burst out angrily, "Oh, I'd have gone—after they got off! But they hung 'round till almost four, and—when I went for my good suit, they—they'd *hid* it—or carried it away! . . . And there was a Christmas tree . . ."

His voice faltered again, while Nancy found herself speechless before what she recognized as a devastating disappointment. She glanced at Scott, coming forward calmly, laying a steady hand on the boy's shoulder. He said—and, knowing what the words cost him, Nancy's heart went out to her husband in adoring gratitude—"Buck up, old scout! We'll have a Christmas tree! And we'll have a party too, you and Mother and I. You can speak your piece and sing your carols for us. And Mother will read us 'The' "—for an appreciable moment Scott's voice faltered, but he went on gamely—" 'The Night Before Christmas.' Did you ever hear it? And I know some stunts that'll make your eyes shine. We'll have our party tomorrow, Christmas Day, sonny; but now"—he was stooping for his overshoes as he spoke—"now we'll go after the tree before it gets too dark! Come on, Mother. We want you, too!"

Mother! Scott hadn't called her that since Jimmy left them! Through tear-blinded eyes Nancy groped for her coat in the diminutive closet. Darkness was coming swiftly as they went into the snowy forest, but they found their tree, and stopped to cut fragrant green branches for decoration. Not till the tree stood proudly in the corner did they remember the lack of tinsel trimmings; but Scott brushed this aside as a mere nothing.

"We've got popcorn, and nothing's prettier. Give us a bit of supper, Nancy, and then I'm going to the village."

"The village! At this hour?"

"You take my sled, mister," cried David, and they saw that his eyes were happy once more, and childlike. "You can coast 'most all the way, like lightning! I'll pop the corn. I'd love to! Boy! It's lucky I milked before I came away!"

The hours that followed passed like magic to Nancy Carson. Veritable wonders were wrought in that small cabin; and oh, it was good to be planning and playing again with a little boy! Not till the child, who had been up since dawn, had dropped asleep on the settee from sheer weariness did she add the finishing touches to the scene.

"It's like a picture of Christmas," she murmured happily. "The tree, so green and slender with its own trimmings, the cone-laden pine at the windows, the bulging stocking at the fireplace, and—and the sleeping boy. I wonder—"

She turned, startled by a step on the creaking snow outside, but it was Scott, of course. He came in silently, not laden with bundles as she'd expected, but empty-handed. There was, she thought, a strange excitement in his manner as he glanced 'round the fire-lit room, his eyes resting for a moment on David's peaceful face. Then he saw the well-filled stocking at the mantel, and his eyes came back unswerving to hers.

"Nancy! Is—is it—?"

She drew nearer, and put her arms around him.

"Yes, dear, it's—Jimmy's—just as we filled it on Christmas Eve three years ago. You see, I couldn't quite bear to leave it behind us when we came away, lying there in his drawer so lonely—at Christmastime. Tell me you don't mind, Scott—won't you? We have our memories, but David—he has so little. That dreadful mother, and—"

Scott cleared his throat, swallowed, and said gently, "He has, I think, the loveliest mother in the world!"

"What do you mean?"

He drew her down onto the settee that faced the sleeping boy and answered, "Listen, Nancy, I went to the schoolhouse. I thought perhaps they'd give me something to trim the tree. The party was over, but the teacher was there with Ira Morse, clearing things away. I told them about David—why he hadn't shown up; and asked some questions. Nancy—what do you think? That Hawkins woman isn't the child's mother! I *knew* it.

"Nobody around here ever saw her. She died when David was a baby, and his father, half-crazed, the natives thought, with grief, brought the child here, and lived like a hermit on the mountain. He died when Dave was about six, and as no one claimed the youngster, and there was no orphan asylum within miles, he was sent to the poor farm, and stayed there until last year, when Clem Hawkins wanted a boy to help do chores, and Dave was the cheapest thing in sight. Guess you wonder where I've been all this time? Well, I've been interviewing the overseer of the poor—destroying red tape by the yard—resorting to bribery and corruption! But— Hello, did I wake you up?"

David roused suddenly, rubbed his eyes. Then, spying the stocking, he wakened thoroughly and asked, "Say! Is— is this Christmas?"

Scott laughed, and glanced at his watch.

"It will be, in twelve minutes. Come here, sonny."

He drew the boy onto his knee and went on quietly: "The stores were closed, David, when I reached the village. I couldn't buy you a Christmas gift, you see. But I thought if we gave you a *real mother* and—and—a *father*—"

"Oh, Scott!"

It was a cry of rapture from Nancy. She had, of course, suspected the ending to his story, but not until that moment had she let herself really believe it. Then, seeing

37

the child's bewilderment, she explained, "He means, dear, that you're our boy now—for always."

David looked up, his brown eyes bugged out with wonder.

"And I needn't go back to Hawkinses'? Not *ever?*"

"Not ever," Scott promised, while his throat tightened at the relief in the boy's voice.

"And I'll have folks, same as the other kids?"

"You've guessed right." The new father spoke lightly in an effort to conceal his feeling. "That is, if you think we'll do!" he added, smiling.

"Oh, you'll—"

Suddenly inarticulate, David turned, throwing his thin arms around Scott's neck in a strangling, boylike hug. Then, a bit ashamed because such things were new to him, he slipped away, standing with his back to them at the window, trying, they saw with understanding hearts, to visualize this unbelievable thing that had come—a miracle—into his starved life. When, after a silence, they joined him, the candle on the table flared up for a protesting moment and then went out. Only starlight and firelight lit the cabin now; and Nancy, peering into the night, said gently, "How beautifully it has cleared. I think I never saw the stars so bright."

"Christmas stars," Scott reminded her and, knowing

the memory that brought the roughness to his voice, she caught and clasped his hand.

It was David who spoke next. He was leaning close to the window, his elbows resting on the sill, his face cupped in his two hands. He seemed to have forgotten them as he said dreamily, "It's Christmas . . . 'Silent night . . . holy night . . .' Like the song. I wonder"—he looked up trustfully into the faces above him—"I wonder if—if maybe one of them stars isn't the Star of Bethlehem!"

A Certain Small Shepherd

❖

REBECCA CAUDILL

This particular story, although only a generation old, is well on its way to becoming a Christmas classic. Once it has been read out loud, most families want it reread again and again, for its message speaks to all of us. It reminds us that we should not ridicule a child and his inward world, for his concept of God's relationship to man may be closer to God's kingdom than is our own.

Rebecca Caudill (1899–?), born in Poor Fork, Kentucky, has never strayed far from her roots. Most of her writing has been centered around the family, around patriotism, around Appalachia. "A Certain Small Shepherd" is one of the all time great read-aloud stories—for children as well as adults—for the words are all simple, the sentences are short, but the rhythm of it is as lovely as a symphony.

This is a story of a strange and marvelous thing. It happened on a Christmas morning, at Hurricane Gap, and not so long ago at that.

But before you hear about Christmas morning, you must hear about Christmas Eve, for that is part of the story.

And before you hear about Christmas Eve, you must hear about Jamie, for without Jamie there would be no story.

Jamie was born on a freakish night in November. The cold that night moved down from the north and rested its heavy hand suddenly on Hurricane Gap. Within an hour's time the naked earth turned brittle. Line Fork Creek froze solid in its winding bed and lay motionless, like a string dropped at the foot of Pine Mountain.

Nothing but the dark wind was abroad in the hollow. Wild creatures huddled in their dens. Cows stood hunched in their stalls. Housewives stuffed the cracks underneath their doors against the needling cold, and men heaped oak and apple wood on their fires.

At the foot of the gap where Jamie's house stood, the wind doubled its fury. It battered the doors of the house. It rattled the windows. It wailed like a banshee in the chimney. "For sure it's bad luck trying to break in," moaned Jamie's mother, and turned her face to her pillow.

"Bad luck has no business here," Jamie's father said bravely. He laid more logs on the fire. Flames licked at them and roared up the chimney. But through the roaring the wind wailed on, thin and high.

Father took the newborn baby from the bed beside its mother and sat holding it on his knee. "Saro," he called, "you and Honey come and see Jamie!"

Two girls came from the shadows of the room. In the firelight they stood looking at the tiny, wrinkled, red face inside the blanket.

"He's such a little brother!" said Saro.

"Give him time, he'll grow," said Father proudly.

"When he's three, he'll be as big as Honey. When he's six, he'll be as big as you. You want to hold him?"

Saro sat down on the stool and Father laid the bundle in her arms.

Honey stood beside Saro. She pulled back the corner of the blanket. She opened one of the tiny hands and laid one of her fingers in it. She smiled at the face in the blanket. She looked upward, smiling at Father.

But Father did not see her. He was standing beside Mother, trying to comfort her.

That night Jamie's mother died.

Jamie ate and slept and grew.

Like other babies, he cut teeth. He learned to sit alone, and to crawl. When he was a year old, he toddled about like other one-year-olds. At two he carried around sticks and stones like other two-year-olds. He threw balls, and built towers of blocks and knocked them down.

Everything that other two-year-olds could do Jamie could do, except one thing. He could not talk.

The women of Hurricane Gap sat in their chimney corners and shook their heads.

"His mother, poor soul, should have rubbed him with lard," said one.

"She ought to have brushed him with a rabbit's foot," said another.

"Wasn't the boy born on a Wednesday?" asked another. " 'Wednesday's child is full of woe,' " she quoted from an old saying.

"Jamie gets everything he wants by pointing," explained Father. "Give him time. He'll learn to talk."

At three Jamie could zip his pants and tie his shoes.

At four he followed Father to the stable and milked the kittens' pan full of milk. But even at four Jamie could not talk like other children. He could only make strange grunting noises.

One day Jamie found a litter of new kittens in a box under the stairs. He ran to the cornfield to tell Father. He wanted to say he had been feeling around in the box for a ball he'd lost, and suddenly his fingers felt something warm and squirmy, and there were all those kittens. But how could you tell somebody something if when you opened your mouth you could only grunt?

Jamie started running. He ran till he reached the orchard. There he threw himself facedown in the tall grass and kicked his feet against the ground.

One day Honey's friend came to play hide-and-seek. Jamie played with them. Because Clive was the oldest, he shut his eyes first and counted to fifty while the other children scattered and hid behind trees in the yard and corners of the house. After he had counted to fifty, the hollow rang with cries.

"One, two, three for Millie!"

"One, two, three for Jamie!"

"One, two, three for Honey!"

"One, two, three—I'm home free."

It came Jamie's turn to shut his eyes. He sat on the doorstep, covered his eyes with his hands, and began to count.

"Listen to Jamie!" Clive called to the other children. The others listened. They all began to laugh.

Jamie got up from the doorstep. He ran after the children. He fought them with both fists and both feet. Honey helped him.

Then Jamie ran away to the orchard and threw himself down on his face in the tall grass and kicked the ground.

Later, when Father was walking through the orchard, he came across Jamie lying in the grass.

"Jamie," said Father, "there's a new calf in the pasture. I need you to help me bring it to the stable."

Jamie got up from the grass. He wiped his eyes. Out of the orchard and across the pasture he trudged at Father's heels. In a far corner of the pasture they found the cow. Beside her, on wobbly legs, stood the new calf.

Together Father and Jamie drove the cow and the calf to the stable, into an empty stall. Together they brought nubbins from the corncrib to feed the cow. Together they made a bed of clean hay for the calf.

"Jamie," said Father the next morning, "I need you to help plow the corn." Father harnessed the horse and lifted Jamie to the horse's back. Away to the cornfield they went, Father walking in front of the horse, Jamie riding, holding tight to the mane.

While Father plowed, Jamie walked in the furrow behind him. When Father lay on his back in the shade of the persimmon tree to rest, Jamie lay beside him. Father told Jamie the names of the birds flying overhead: the turkey vulture lifting and tilting its uplifted wings against the white clouds, the carrion crow flapping lazily and sailing, and the sharp-shinned hawk gliding to rest in the woodland.

The next day Jamie helped Father set out sweet potatoes. Other days he helped Father trim fencerows and mend fences. Whatever Father did, Jamie helped him.

One day Father drove the car out of the shed and stopped in front of the house. "Jamie!" he called. "Jump in. We're going across Pine Mountain."

"Can I go too?" asked Honey.

"Not today," said Father. "I'm taking Jamie to see a doctor."

The doctor looked at Jamie's throat. He listened to Jamie grunt. He shook his head.

"You might see Dr. Jones," he said.

Father and Jamie got into the car and drove across Big Black Mountain to see Dr. Jones.

"Maybe Jamie could learn to talk," said Dr. Jones. "But he would have to be sent away to a special school. He would have to stay there several months. He might even have to stay two or three years. Or four."

"It is a long time," said Dr. Jones.

"And the pocket is empty," said Father.

So Father and Jamie got into the car and started home. Usually Father talked to Jamie as they drove along. Now they drove all the way, across Big Black and across Pine, without a word.

In August every year, school opened at Hurricane Gap. On the first morning of school, the year that Jamie was six, Father handed him a book, a tablet, a pencil, and a box of crayons, all shiny and new.

"You're going to school, Jamie," he said. "I'll go with you this morning."

The neighbors watched them walking down the road together, toward the little one-room schoolhouse.

"Poor, foolish Father!" they said, and shook their heads. "Trying to make somebody out of that no-account boy!"

Miss Creech, the teacher, shook her head too. With so many children, so many classes, so many grades, she hadn't time for a boy that couldn't talk, she told Father.

"What will Jamie do all day long?" she asked.

"He will listen," said Father.

So Jamie took his tablet, his pencil, and his box of crayons, and sat down in an empty seat in the front row.

Every day Jamie listened. He learned the words in the pages of his book. He learned how to count. He liked the reading and counting. But the part of school Jamie liked best was the big piece of paper Miss Creech gave him every day. On it he printed words in squares, like the other children. He wrote numbers. He drew pictures and colored them with his crayons. He could say things on paper.

One day Miss Creech said Jamie had the best paper in the first grade. She held it up for all the children to see.

On sunny days on the playground the children played ball games and three-deep and duck-on-a-rock—games a boy can play without talking. On rainy days they played indoors.

One rainy day the children played a guessing game. Jamie knew the answer that no other child could guess. But he couldn't say the answer. He didn't know how to spell the answer. He could only point to show that he knew the answer.

That evening at home he threw his book into the corner. He slammed the door. He pulled Honey's hair. He twisted the cat's tail. The cat yowled and leaped under the bed.

"Jamie," said Father, "cats have feelings, just like boys."

Every year the people of Hurricane Gap celebrated Christmas in the white-steepled church that stood across the road from Jamie's house. On Christmas Eve the boys and girls gave a Christmas play. People came miles to see it, from the other side of Pine Mountain and from the head of every creek and hollow. Miss Creech directed the play.

Through the late fall, as the leaves fell from the trees and the days grew shorter and the air snapped with cold, Jamie wondered when Miss Creech would talk about the play. Finally, one afternoon in November, Miss Creech announced it was time to begin play practice.

50

Jamie laid his book inside the desk and listened carefully as Miss Creech assigned the parts of the play.

Miss Creech gave the part of Mary to Joan, who lived up Pine Mountain, beyond the rock quarry. She asked Honey to bring her big doll to be the baby. She gave the part of Joseph to Henry, who lived at the head of Little Laurelpatch. She asked Saro to be an angel, Clive the innkeeper. She chose three big boys to be people living in Bethlehem. The rest of the boys and girls would sing carols, she said.

Jamie for a moment listened to the sound of the words he had heard. Yes, Miss Creech expected him to sing carols.

Every day after school the boys and girls went with Miss Creech up the road to the church and practiced the Christmas play.

Every day Jamie stood in the front row of the carolers. The first day he stood quietly. The second day he shoved Milly, who was standing next to him. The third day he pulled Honey's hair. The fourth day, when the carolers began singing, Jamie ran to the window, grabbed a ball from the sill, and bounced it across the floor.

"Wait a minute, children," Miss Creech said to the children. She turned to Jamie.

"Jamie," she asked, "how would you like to be a shepherd?"

"He's too little," said one of the big shepherds.

"No, he isn't," said Saro. "If my father was a shepherd, Jamie would help him."

That afternoon Jamie became a small shepherd. He ran home after practice to tell Father. Father couldn't understand what Jamie was telling him, but he knew that Jamie had been changed into somebody important.

One afternoon at play practice, Miss Creech said to the boys and girls, "Forget you are Joan and Henry and Saro and Clive and Jamie. Remember that you are Mary and Joseph, an angel, an innkeeper, and a shepherd, and that strange things are happening in the hollow where you live."

That night at bedtime, Father took the big Bible off the table. Saro and Honey and Jamie gathered around the fire. Over the room a hush fell as Father read: " 'And there were in the same country shepherds abiding in the field, keeping watch over their flock by night. And, lo, the angel of the Lord came upon them, and the glory of the Lord shone around about them: and they were sore afraid. And the angel said unto them, Fear not: for, behold, I bring you good tidings of great joy, which shall be to all people. . . . And it came to pass, as the angels were gone away from them into heaven, the shepherds said to one another, Let us now go even unto Bethlehem, and see this thing which is come to pass, which the Lord hath made known unto us. And they came with haste, and found Mary, and Joseph, and the babe lying in a manger.' "

Christmas drew near. At home in the evenings, when they had finished studying their lessons, the boys and girls of Hurricane Gap made decorations for the Christmas tree that would stand in the church. They glued together strips of bright-colored paper in long chains. They whittled stars and baby lambs and camels out of wild cherry wood. They strung long strings of popcorn.

Jamie strung a string of popcorn. Every night as Father read from the Bible, Jamie added more kernels to his string.

"Jamie, are you trying to make a string long enough to reach to the top of Pine Mountain?" asked Honey one night.

Jamie did not hear her. He was far away on a hillside, tending sheep. And even though he was a small shepherd and could only grunt when he tried to talk, an angel wrapped around with dazzling light was singling him out to tell him a wonderful thing had happened down in the hollow in a cow stall. He fell asleep, stringing his popcorn and listening.

In a corner of the room where the fire burned, Father pulled from under his bed the trundle bed in which Jamie slept. He turned back the covers, picked Jamie up from the floor, and laid him gently in the bed.

The next day Father went across Pine Mountain to the store. When he came home, he handed Saro a package. In it was cloth of four colors: green, gold, white, and red.

"Make Jamie a shepherd's coat, like the picture in the Bible," Father said to Saro.

Father went into the woods and found a crooked limb of a tree. He made it into a shepherd's crook for Jamie.

Jamie went to school the next morning carrying his shepherd's crook and his shepherd's coat on his arm. He would wear his coat and carry his crook when the boys and girls practiced the play.

All day Jamie waited patiently to practice the play. All day he sat listening. But who could tell whose voice he heard? It might have been Miss Creech's. It might have been an angel's.

Two days before Christmas, Jamie's father and Clive's father drove in a pickup truck along Trace Branch Road, looking for a Christmas tree. On the mountainside they spotted a juniper growing broad and tall and free. With axes they cut it down. They snaked it down the mountainside and loaded it into the truck.

Father had opened the doors of the church wide to get the tree inside. It reached to the ceiling. Frost-blue berries shone on its feathery green branches. The air around it smelled of spice.

That afternoon the mothers of Hurricane Gap, and Miss Creech, and all the boys and girls gathered at the church to decorate the tree.

In the tip-top of the tree they fastened the biggest star. Among the branches they hung other stars, and baby lambs and the camels whittled out of wild cherry wood. They hung chains from branch to branch. Last of all, they festooned the tree with strings of snowy popcorn.

"Ah!" they said, as they stood back and looked at the tree. "Ah!"

Beside the tree the boys and girls practiced the Christmas play for the last time. When they had finished, they started home. Midway down the aisle they turned and looked again at the tree.

Saro opened the door. "Look!" she called, "Look, everybody! It's snowing!"

Jamie, the next morning, looked out on a world

such as he had never seen. Hidden were the roads and the fences, the woodpile and the swing under the oak tree, all buried deep under a lumpy quilt of snow. And before a stinging wind, snowflakes still madly whirled and danced.

Saro and Honey joined Jamie at the window.

"You can't see across Line Fork Creek in this storm," said Saro. "And where is Pine Mountain?"

"Where is the church?" asked Honey. "That's what I'd like to know."

Jamie turned to them with questions in his eyes.

"If it had been snowing hard that night in Bethlehem, Jamie," Honey told him, "the shepherds wouldn't have had their sheep out in the pasture. They would have had them in the stable, keeping them warm, wouldn't they, Father? They wouldn't have heard what the angel said, all shut indoors like that."

"When angels have something to tell a shepherd," said Father, "they can find him in any place, in any sort of weather. If the shepherd is listening, he will hear."

At eleven o'clock the telephone rang.

"Hello!" said Father.

Saro and Honey and Jamie heard Miss Creech's voice, "I've just got the latest weather report. This storm is going on all day, and into the night. Do you think—"

The telephone started ringing, and once it started to ring it wouldn't stop. Everyone in Hurricane Gap listened. The news they heard was always bad. Drifts ten feet high were piled up along Trace Branch Road. The boys and girls in Little Laurelpatch couldn't get out. Joseph lived in Little Laurelpatch. The road up to the rock quarry . . . Mary couldn't get down the mountain. And then the telephone went silent, dead in the storm.

Meanwhile, the snow kept up its crazy dance before the wind. It drifted in great white mounds across the roads and in the fencerows.

"Nobody but a foolish man would take to the road on a day like this," said Father.

At dinner Jamie sat at the table staring at his plate.

"Shepherds must eat, Jamie," said Father.

"Honey and I don't feel like eating either, Jamie," said Saro, "but see how Honey is eating!"

Still Jamie stared at his plate.

"Know what?" asked Saro. "Because we're all disappointed, we won't save the Christmas stack cake for tomorrow. We'll have a slice today. As soon as you eat your dinner, Jamie."

Still Jamie stared at his plate. He did not touch his food.

"You think that play was real, don't you, Jamie?" said Honey. "It wasn't real. It was just a play we were giving, like some story we'd made up."

Jamie could hold his sobs no longer. His body heaved as he ran to Father. Father laid an arm about Jamie's shoulders.

"Sometimes, Jamie," he said, "angels say to shepherds, 'Be of good courage.' "

On through the short afternoon the storm raged. Father heaped more wood on the fire. Saro sat in front of the fire reading a book. Honey cracked hickory nuts on the stone hearth. Jamie sat.

"Bring the popper, Jamie, and I'll pop some corn for you," said Father.

Jamie shook his head.

"Want me to read to you?" asked Saro.

Jamie shook his head.

"Why don't you help Honey crack hickory nuts?" asked Father.

Jamie shook his head.

"Jamie still thinks he's a shepherd," said Honey.

After a while Jamie left the fire and stood at the window, watching the wild storm. He squinted his eyes and

58

stared—he motioned to his Father to come and look. Saro and Honey, too, hurried to the window and peered out.

Through the snowdrifts trudged a man, followed by a woman. They were bundled and buttoned from head to foot, and their faces were lowered against the wind and the flying snowflakes.

"Lord, have mercy!" said Father as he watched them turn in at the gate.

Around the house the man and woman made their way to the back door. As Father opened the door to them, a gust of snow-laden wind whisked into the kitchen.

"Come in out of the cold," said Father.

The man and the woman stepped inside. They stamped their feet on the kitchen floor and brushed the snow from their clothes. They followed Father into the front room and sat down before the fire in the chairs Father told Saro to bring. Father, too, sat down.

Jamie stood beside Father. Saro and Honey stood behind his chair. The three of them stared at the man and the woman silently.

"Where did you come from?" asked Father.

"The other side of Pine Mountain," said the man.

"Why didn't you stop sooner?" said Father.

"We did stop," the man said. "At three houses. Nobody had room," he said.

Father was silent for a minute. He looked at his own bed and at Jamie's trundle bed underneath it. The man and the woman looked numbly into the fire.

"How far were you going?" asked Father.

"Down Straight Creek," said the man. He jerked his head toward the woman. "To her sister's."

"You'll never get there tonight," Father said.

"Maybe——" said the man. "Maybe there'd be a place in your stable."

"We could lay pallets on the kitchen floor," said Father.

The woman looked at the children. She shook her head. "The stable is better," she said.

"The stable is cold," said Father.

"It will do," said the woman.

When the man and the woman had dried their clothes and warmed themselves, Father led the way to the stable. He carried an armload of quilts and on top of them an old buffalo skin. From his right arm swung a lantern and a milk bucket. "I'll milk while I'm there," he said to Saro. "Get supper ready."

Jamie and Saro and Honey watched from the kitchen window as the three trudged through the snowdrifts to the stable.

It was dark when Father came back to the house.

"How long are the man and woman going to stay?" asked Honey.

Father hung a teakettle of water on the crane over the fire and went upstairs to find another lantern.

"All night tonight," he said as he came down the stairs. "Maybe longer."

Father hurriedly ate the supper Saro put on the table. Then he took in one hand the lighted lantern and a tin bucket filled with supper for the man and the woman.

"I put some Christmas stack cake in the bucket," said Saro.

In his other hand, Father took the teakettle.

"It's cold in that stable," he said as he started out the kitchen door. "Bitter cold."

On the doorstep he turned. "Don't wait up for me," he called back. "I may be gone a good while."

Over the earth darkness thickened. Still the wind blew and the snow whirled. The clock on the mantel struck eight. It ticked solemnly in the quiet house where Saro and Honey and Jamie waited.

"Why doesn't Father come?" complained Honey.

"Why don't you hang up your stocking and go to bed?" asked Saro. "Jamie, it's time to hang up your stocking, too, and go to bed."

Jamie did not answer. He sat staring into the fire.

"That Jamie! He still thinks he's a shepherd," said Honey as she hung her stocking under the mantel.

"Jamie," said Saro, "aren't you going to hang up your stocking and go to bed?" She pulled the trundle bed from beneath Father's bed and turned back the covers. She turned back the covers on Father's bed. She hung up her stocking and followed Honey upstairs.

"Jamie!" she called out.

Still Jamie stared into the fire. A strange feeling was growing inside him. This night was not like other nights, he knew. Something mysterious was going on. He felt afraid.

What was that he heard? The wind? Only the wind?

He lay down on the bed with his clothes on. He dropped off to sleep. A rattling at the door wakened him.

He sat upright quickly. He looked around. His heart beat fast. But nothing in the room had changed. Everything was as it had been when he lay down. The fire was burning, two stockings, Saro's and Honey's, hung under the mantel, the clock was ticking solemnly.

He looked at Father's bed. The sheets were just as Saro had turned them back.

There! There it was again! It sounded like singing. "Glory to God! On earth peace!"

Jamie breathed hard. Had he heard that? Or had he only said it to himself? He lay down again and pulled the quilts over his head.

"Get up, Jamie," he heard Father saying. "Put your clothes on quick."

Jamie opened his eyes. He saw daylight filling the room. He saw Father standing over him, bundled in warm clothes.

Wondering, Jamie flung the quilts back and rolled out of bed.

"Why, Jamie," said Father, "you're already dressed!"

Father went to the stairs. "Saro! Honey!" he called. "Come quick!"

"What's happened, Father?" asked Saro.

"What are we going to do?" asked Honey as she fumbled sleepily with her shoelaces.

"Come with me," said Father.

"Where are we going?" asked Honey.

"To the stable?" asked Saro.

"The stable was no fit place," said Father. "Not when

63

the church was close by, and it with a stove in it, and coal for burning."

Out into the cold, silent, white morning they went. The wind had died. The clouds were lifting. One star in the vast sky, its brilliance fading in the growing light, shone down on Hurricane Gap.

Father led the way through the drifted snow. The others followed, stepping in his tracks. As Father pushed open the church door, the fragrance of the Christmas tree rushed out at them. The potbellied stove glowed red with the fire within.

Muffling his footsteps, Father walked quietly up the aisle. Wonderingly, the others followed. There, beside the star-crowned Christmas tree where the Christmas play was to have been given, they saw the woman. She lay on the old buffalo skin, covered with quilts. Beside her pallet sat the man.

The woman smiled at them. "You came to see?" she asked, and lifted the cover.

Saro went first and peeped under the cover. Honey went next.

"You look, too, Jamie," said Saro.

For a moment Jamie hesitated. He leaned forward and took one quick look. Then he turned, shot down the aisle and out of the church, slamming the door behind him.

Saro ran down the church aisle, calling after him.

"Wait, Saro," said Father, watching Jamie through the window.

To the house Jamie made his way, half running along the path Father's big boots had cut through the snowdrifts.

Inside the house he hurriedly pulled his shepherd's robe over his coat. He snatched up his crook from the chimney corner.

With his hand on the doorknob, he glanced toward the fireplace. There, under the mantel, hung Saro's and Honey's stockings. And there, beside them, hung his stocking! Now who had hung it there? It had in it the same bulge his stocking had had every Christmas morning since he could remember, a bulge made by an orange.

Jamie ran to the fireplace and felt the toe of his stocking. Yes, there was the dime, just as on other Christmas mornings.

Hurriedly he emptied his stocking. With the orange and the dime in one hand and the crook in the other, he made his way toward the church. Father and Saro, still watching, saw his shepherd's robe—a spot of glowing color in a great white world.

Father opened the church door.

Without looking to the left or right, Jamie hurried up

the aisle. Father and Saro followed him. Beside the pallet he dropped to his knees.

"Here is a Christmas gift for the child," he said, clear and strong.

"Father!" gasped Saro. "Father, listen to Jamie!"

The woman turned back the covers from the baby's face. Jamie gently laid the orange beside the baby's tiny hand.

"And here's a gift for the mother," Jamie said to the woman. He put the dime in her hand.

"Surely," the woman spoke softly, "the Lord lives this day."

"Surely," said Father, "the Lord does live this day, and all days. And He is loving and merciful and good."

In the hush that followed, Christmas in all its joys and its majesty came to Hurricane Gap. And it wasn't so long ago at that.

Christmas Is for Families

LOIS HANSEN

How often we needlessly worry about furnishings in a house, as we anticipate the arrival of company we have to impress, only to discover that the love manifested in the home creates a magic mist that gilds everything far more than any number of priceless antiques ever could have. This particular story—written by a cherished friend of our family—has long been a favorite of ours, for it portrays just such a . . . not a house, but a home.

Lois Hansen and her husband, Ted, today live on the shores of Lake Lucerne in Northern California. Only a few weeks ago, they phoned me, telling me of how my bringing back her almost-forty-year-old story has incredibly enriched their lives today. And how joyful they are that the story lives on!

Martha Dean wrestled with her problem all during the confusion that was the usual family breakfast.

As she toasted and stirred and fried to please each individual taste, she was only partly conscious of the family talk that rolled on about her. Her mind was far away, and yet so automatic had this early morning task become that her busy hands moved of their own accord, leaving her mind free to work on all angles of her bothersome problem.

At last the minor crises had all been solved. Her husband, Jim, had found his lost letter, Jimmie was assured that he really must wear his raincoat, and a stamp was magically produced for Jill. Jimmie was the last to go, and as the door banged shut behind his hurrying feet, Martha lifted baby Petey into his high chair and began to spoon cereal into his open mouth.

Petey looked at his mother and chuckled as though it was all very funny.

Martha smiled back at her youngest son, but worriedly. "It's really no joke, son. I don't know what to do. The problem seems to get bigger all the time. If your big brother Larry hadn't married a girl who has always had everything, maybe I wouldn't take it so hard. But with all Fran has been used to, how can I ask her and Larry to come and visit in this old house? And yet, if Larry doesn't come home for Christmas—"

Martha paused. There was Jill, too. Maybe it was a blessing in disguise that her boyfriend, Bob, wanted her to come up to his folks' cabin for the skiing. He might fall out of love with her if he saw how her family lived.

Martha looked at the pile of breakfast dishes and winced a little.

"Come on, Petey," she said with sudden decision. "Let's go on a tour of this monstrosity and see if anything can be done in the next few weeks to turn the place into a dream house, so I can feel up to inviting my sophisticated older children and their wealthy partners home for Christmas."

"Cwistmas," Petey gurgled as his mother buttoned him into a red sweater and went out into the fresh morning air.

Martha walked along the old-fashioned brick walk.

I needn't be ashamed of my garden anyway, she thought.

The rich purple of the cinerias and primroses made a lovely frame for the green of the lawn. A few new blossoms were appearing on the stocks, and the poinsettia bush made a charming picture against the white wall.

If we could just be like Adam and Eve and have gardens without houses, Martha thought.

She turned at the gate and tried to pretend that she was seeing the house through Fran's and Bob's eyes. They were, after all, the ones who would notice its shabby appearance most. Larry and Jill had grown up here. They knew the old place by heart. But of course they might see its shabbiness in an entirely new light, now that they had become familiar with such lovely homes.

Martha's gray eyes traveled over the object of her concern. No. It would never do. The great sprawling mass was of no particular period. The upper story sat primly in the center of the roof like a spinster's best hat. The many windows were high and small. *Something like those old-fashioned glasses my Uncle George used to wear.* She smiled in remembrance.

The white paint glistened in occasional spurts of sunshine and the front screen door was tipped at a rather rakish angle, as if it had been slammed too often and too hard by little people who were in a real hurry to get outside.

And that backyard. Martha closed her eyes and wished she could as easily dispose of the backyard problem. But the sweet peas planted against the side of the garage would be lovely in the spring and would help to soften the picture.

Just in time, Petey was rescued from a puddle left by the recent rain. His hand nestled warmly into Martha's as she said, "Let's go upstairs, Pete, and see the ocean, and in the meantime try to discover some magic to turn those worn old bedrooms into some like they have in magazine pictures."

On the upstairs landing they paused for a moment, and Martha caught her breath at the wealth of beauty spread all about her. "This particular stretch of the Pacific Ocean must be the loveliest place in the whole world," she said to herself.

The lacy branches of the eucalyptus trees at the edge of the lagoon made patterns against the gray of the sky, and farther out against the edge of the cliff the ocean sprawled and rolled, sending its fountains of spray high in the air.

Turning into the narrow hall, Martha opened each door in turn, and shut it again almost as quickly.

Jim's long sick spell and the trip East for Larry's wedding, coming so close together, had taken all they had saved for remodeling these rooms.

Downstairs again, Martha tied on her old apron and mentally counted her blessings as she started the breakfast dishes at last.

"I guess a person can't have everything, and Jim's being well is worth more than a whole tract of houses."

That night Martha talked the problem over with Jim.

"If I could just have new curtains for the living room," she sighed. "These give the outside of the house such a forlorn look."

"I know, honey, and I wish you could, too," he answered. "But everything seems to come due at Christmas— taxes, insurance—everything. This year we have Jill's trip to manage, too. Maybe next year."

Martha nodded. "I suppose so. But it would be so wonderful to have the house fixed up and all the children under the same roof again."

"Fathers have their lonesome moments, too," Jim answered. "Maybe I don't always say very much, but I remember well enough when Larry and Jill were small, and wish it could be that way this year. But, honey, if we do have them come, it will have to be with the house just as it is."

In the weeks that followed, Christmas trees began to appear on the street corners. Lights began to glow in the store windows, parents went shopping with eager little boys and girls, and even the old house took on a festive air.

Wreaths hung in the downstairs windows, and the big tree that Jim and Jimmie brought in from the hills glowed with lights and wore its ancient ornaments proudly.

The big kitchen began to come alive with the sounds and smells of Christmas. Everyone helped crack the nuts for the cookies and fruitcake Martha sent to Fran and Larry. Jars were filled with nuts and candies for gifts. The recipes Martha's grandmother had used were used again.

Petey got in everyone's way and was hugged and kissed a hundred times a day. Snatches of carols floated out of the house as Jill taught the two little boys the same old songs she and Larry had learned, meanwhile walking on a rosy cloud as the days grew fewer and fewer till she would see her Bob again.

The day before Christmas, the gift came from Fran and Larry. Martha's heart turned over as she took the wrappings off a magnificent picture of Jesus and His disciples on the way to Emmaus.

"Oh, Mother!" Jill gasped.

"Sa-a-ay! That's all right," Jim said, admiring the painting.

"Where'll we hang it, Mom?" the always-practical Jimmie wondered.

Petey just chuckled as he wrapped the tissue from the box around his head and urged everyone to play peekaboo.

"Did you know about this, Jill?" Martha asked with a knowing glance.

"No, I didn't, Mother, but isn't it beautiful?"

"It's what I've always wanted," Martha sighed happily. "Wasn't it sweet of them. And yet"—her eyes were wistful—"I wish they could be here to enjoy it with us."

"Hey!" Jim shouted with a quick glance at the clock. "Was someone supposed to catch a train? Look at the time, Jill!"

"Oh, Dad, Bob would have a fit if I missed it. We had planned to stay with his folks tonight and go on to Tahoe with the crowd tomorrow."

"Sounds like fun," Martha said on the way to the station. "We'll miss our girl on Christmas, but judging from the stars in your eyes, your Christmas will be a very happy one."

The house was quiet after Jill had left. Martha and Jim read the old, loved Christmas stories to the little boys and helped them hang up the all-important Christmas stockings. And when the family were all in bed, Martha shed a few quick tears as she said a special prayer for the ones who weren't home this Christmas Eve.

The sound of bells awakened them on Christmas morning. Martha lay quietly listening to their message, before a shout from the living room brought her to her feet. Jimmie had found his Erector set and Petey was running his new wagon around and around, finding a few new places to scratch on the shabby furniture.

After breakfast, Jim took the boys to the beach and Martha cleared out mountains of tissue, trying not to feel sorry for herself. The activities involved in getting Christmas dinner for three hungry people kept her mind off her lonesomeness.

The little boys returned from the beach, and, tired from their play, took a nap before dinner. Jim sat in the sudden quiet, reading the news magazines he scarcely had time to see on work days.

"Peace—it's wonderful." Jim grinned at Martha as she stole time from her cooking for a small rest on his lap and a Christmas kiss.

"Doesn't the house look nice, dear? Christmas things hide a lot, and no one will ever see the scratches anymore. They won't have eyes for anything but our beautiful picture." Martha's glance lingered possessively on the scene as she spoke.

"Like it, Mommy?" Jim asked. "I thought the card that came with it was a beauty, too."

"It was. But you know what I wish, don't you, Jim?"

"Of course I do! You, my dear, are incurably a mother, and if your chicks aren't with you, your feathers droop."

The table was delightful with Jill's centerpiece of a fat red candle and Christmas greens. The beautifully ironed linen cloth was an old one that had worn thin in the twenty-five years since Martha had been a bride. And Jimmie had polished the old silver until the satiny finish reflected the soft candle glow.

The crisp brown of the nut loaf flanked by the tiny creamed onions and a mound of fluffy mashed potatoes, along with home-canned pickles and Martha's own special fruit salad, caused Jim to heave a great hungry sigh as he buckled Petey into his high chair and sat down at the head of the table.

"Enough food here for an army, dear. You are going to have to remember that your family is getting smaller all the time."

Martha smiled, and glanced around the table to be sure everything was in order. She was glad that Jimmie had washed his hands and face without being told.

The little boys bowed their heads, and their father's deep voice asked God to "Bless our food, and those who are not with us, and keep them safe today."

And when the amen was said, Petey's ready smile broke through the moment of longing as he reached out both fat hands for the "Tatoes, pease!"

"Jim, did that sound like a car to you?" Martha paused in the act of filling Petey's plate.

"I didn't hear anything," Jim answered. "Jimmie, do you want to go and see?"

Jimmie's eyes were like saucers in his round freckled face as he rushed back from his trip to the front door.

"Daddy! Mother! They're all here!"

Martha had half risen from her place, but it was Jim who spoke. "Who, son?"

"Jill and Larry and Fran, and that guy Jill went to see." But Martha was halfway to the front door, and Larry's eager arms were around his mother's waist, with Fran close beside.

As Martha turned to Jill, the girl said shyly, "This is Bob, Mother." Martha's eyes liked what they saw.

Jim had never looked so happy as when his tall son slapped his shoulder and told him how glad they were to be home.

Jimmie danced about like a wild Indian, and only his mother's reproving glance kept him from uttering an original war cry. Petey ran to get his new red wagon and bring it to Fran for her approval.

The dinner was marvelous, the children said, and Fran seemed to enjoy it most of all. Jimmie and Bob found a common interest in model planes, and Jimmie had another hero besides Larry.

The big log crackled in the fireplace after the dishes were done, and then Martha and Jim heard the whole story.

"It all began with Jill," Larry said. "She wrote us after Thanksgiving and told us why Mother didn't feel like she could ask us to come home Christmas."

"Oh, Jill!" Martha said faintly, and blushed to the roots of her graying hair.

"Well, of course," said Jill, "Mother was embarrassed about the old house, but I just told Fran that when she saw the warmth and love pouring out of every crack of the old place, she wouldn't even notice the shabbiness."

"That's my girl," said Bob. "Does everyone see now why I love her?"

"We know better than anyone else why, I think, Bob," Jim said after the laugh that followed Bob's impulsiveness.

"But the lovely picture!" Martha turned to Fran. "Why did you send it if you were coming?"

"Jill's letter came the day we sent the gift," Fran answered, "and Larry got plane reservations at once." Fran looked at Larry. "It took a special kind of home to give me a husband as loving and thoughtful as Larry, and I'm so glad I belong to it, too."

"We're glad, too," Martha said. Then she turned to Bob. "But there's another mystery. I thought you and Jill were going to Tahoe for the skiing. How do you happen to be so far from there?"

"Simple as anything. When Jill told me she had heard from Fran, and that they were coming, well, I knew she wanted to be with her family. So here we are." Bob smiled. "There will be skiing till May, but only one Christmas all year."

"Will you play for us, Mother, while we sing the carols?" Larry suggested.

"Oh, no! I can't, Larry. I don't practice anymore and

81

I make so many mistakes. In fact, Jill told me the other day that I'm the only person she knows who can play each hand in a different key."

Everybody laughed.

"But we want you to do it just like the old days," Larry begged.

Martha played them all, from "We Three Kings" to "Jingle Bells." The old house seemed to fold them close as the young voices rose and fell in the Christmas melodies. Even Petey's baby voice shrilled out bravely in "Silent Night, Holy Night."

At last the fire in the fireplace burned low and evening prayers brought the little group close together.

Fran and Larry went up the stairs to Larry's old room, and Bob was given a room where he could hear the waves breaking on the shore and dream of the time when he and Jill would know the same happiness as Jill's parents.

Two o'clock in the morning. The old house was quiet again. Jim woke with a start. Martha was not beside him. He sat up. Where could she be? For twenty-five years he had always been able to reach out and touch her at night. Then he remembered and sank back again on his pillows. The children were all home, and Martha was probably up to her old tricks, roaming around to see if they were all right.

Upstairs, Martha stood for a moment outside the room of her son and the girl he loved. Their even breathing told her all was well.

The old bed in Bob's room creaked restlessly. *Dreaming of Jill, no doubt,* Martha thought. *It would be nice to have the wedding in June.*

Downstairs, Jill's dark head was turned slightly on her pillow, the hand with the watch from Bob tucked under her cheek.

Jimmie would never stay covered up, and Martha smoothed the tumbled blankets and kissed him lightly.

In his crib, Petey slept like a Christmas angel, the moonlight forming a halo about his golden head.

Martha crept quietly back to bed.

"They're almost all grown up, Mommy," Jim teased her gently. "You needn't cover them up all the rest of their lives."

Martha sighed happily. "Oh, Jim, was there ever such a lovely, lovely family? Houses don't really matter. It's the love in them that counts."

The Real Christmas Spirit

✤

HELEN E. RICHARDS

Traditions are not necessarily static, unchanging. They can become boring and stuffy. There may come times when a bit of freshness is needed. Improvisation more likely will bring vitality than will Christmas-as-usual.

Well, in the case of the Davenports, Christmas-as-usual was out of the question—so what then?

In a prosperous Middle Western town, on the east side, at the upper end of a long avenue of comfortable homes, the street veers suddenly to the right and ends in Cedar Hill, a blind but beautiful alley, bordered with lawns, decorated at this time of year with strange, nobby figures of gunnysacking wound with cord and with piles of straw overlaid with boards. Back of these suggestions of the landscape gardener stand four houses, wide-spreading, luxurious—Cedar Hill homes of the Davenports, the Clydes, the Lees, and the Ludingtons.

On Christmas Eve it was the custom for Cordelia Davenport to give a recital, and the Clydes and the Lees and the Ludingtons came laden with their articles of commerce, and hung them on the Davenport Christmas tree at the end of a long drawing room. The little group of families on Cedar Hill always celebrated royally, because it was within the power of Cedar Hill residents to do so.

"And Cedar Hill leads the town," quoted James Davenport, Jr., to his sister.

James Jr. was taller than his father, and he carried himself with a regal air in spite of his extreme youth. He drew down the library shades and flung himself into an armchair.

"Sis, what do you say to going to Meredith's for programs? They have some gorgeous new leather things. I say white morocco, with the Davenport coat of arms in gold and blue. How does that strike you?"

"And mistletoe instead of holly. Borts are taking orders now," supplemented Sis. "And I want Mother to try that new caterer on West Fifth. They say he is so much better than—" She stopped suddenly and looked up at James with a startled expression. Both listened intently. They heard the voice of their mother talking to James Sr. in the music room.

"It isn't right, James, with all the financial reverses you have suffered this year and all the calls there are for charity, that we should spend so lavishly. I shall never forget how nearly we came to losing the old home itself. We ought not to have any recital at all!"

"No recital!" James Sr. gasped. "What will the Ludingtons say?" he cried.

"The Ludingtons can be thankful that they live in well-favored America, and not in starving Germany."

James Jr. slipped from his chair and caught his sister's arm.

87

"What is it?" he whispered. "What are they talking about?"

"Hush!"

James Sr. was speaking again. "We can manage the recital, I think, Cordelia, and have something to give besides," he said in a low, generous voice.

"Then we ought to give twice as much, and go without the recital," insisted Mrs. Davenport. "It would be positively wicked for us to have the usual orgy of presents and feasting while there is such great need. The Davenports have always led. Let us lead now, in giving—in sacrifice."

"What will the children say?" asked her husband suddenly.

"Never mind what they say, James. They need just this kind of experience. They are spendthrifts, both of them. Jim Jr. hasn't the first notion of the value of money, and as for Sis—we've encouraged her in—oh, well, never mind. We always had more than enough, until the stock company failed. Perhaps it hasn't been best not to let them know about our worries," she added thoughtfully.

Sis gazed at her brother solemnly. "Are we that bad, Jim?" she questioned under her breath.

He was silent. The fire in the grate crackled and snapped and leaped and fell. The voices in the music room had dropped to a lower key.

"What about stock failing?" James Jr. asked finally. "I heard rumors at college, but I didn't suppose it was really so, when Dad didn't mention anything."

James Jr. slung himself forward, resting his chin in his hands. Sis watched him in silence.

"We'll let the morocco programs go—eh, Sis?" He laughed shortly. Then he looked up. "See here. How much money have you?"

"Not more than five dollars, I guess. I spent the rest for—"

"And I haven't a cent!"

Sis gazed at him tremulously. "We can't have any Christmas," she faltered.

James Jr. stood up. In the firelight, against the dark background of the library, he loomed like a young giant, his features standing out white, vivid, forceful, with all the Davenport pride and reserve. Quietly he put his hands in his pockets and stared into the fire.

"We have always led, Sis, as Mother says," he said slowly, "and our house has always been gay at Christmastime. We have to keep it up!"

"But the money, Jim— If we—"

"We can celebrate Christmas without money, Sis.

What's family pride for? It isn't money pride, Sis, it's the real article. We'll have our party just the same. And we'll do it on what money we can scare up between us!"

The time had been, years before, when the Cedar Hill families were poor, when the Davenport Christmas party had been very gay but very economical. But of late years, money and social rivalry had increased the expenditure and stunted the gaiety. Cordelia Davenport had been the leader, and if sometimes she sighed for more sincerity and less show in their social affairs, still it had not occurred to her that the situation could be remedied. So used had she become to professional singers and high-priced caterers that to forego these luxuries, even from a sense of duty, meant no Christmas festivity, and she sighed as she thought how they would miss the annual gathering.

James Sr., too, much as he hated the stately social functions, began to realize a loss as the holidays approached.

"No Christmas this year," he said with a shrug as he met Mr. Clyde at the corner and they turned toward Cedar Hill for dinner.

"That's all right," declared Clyde seriously. "We're cutting out some things, too. Rather hard on the children."

Silently the two men strode on up the hill, and it did

not occur to either of them that they could celebrate without an outlay.

"What can you do without money?" asked Davenport gloomily.

"I know," nodded Clyde. "It doesn't rain Christmas doings—you have to buy them."

It was a few days before Christmas, and Cordelia Davenport was making her afternoon toilet before a tall mirror in her dressing room. Tall mirrors were rather a specialty with her, and if any one of her family wished to give her an expensive present, he knew without asking that she could find space somewhere for another mirror—or for a cut-glass candlestick. She was not sure which of these she liked best. James Jr. once said that his mother ought to live in a glass house.

Today, as Mrs. Davenport dressed, she saw reflected in her mirror the figure of a woman crossing the street and aiming straight for her front door. It was a portly figure, increased to absurdity by a huge collaret and a muff the size of two Angora cats.

"Madam Ludington!" exclaimed Cordelia. "What can she possibly want?"

This question did not imply that Madam's calls were infrequent, but merely that her movements were sometimes social maneuvers. The recent stricture in the Christmas expenditure of the Davenports altered the social opportunities.

"It is so lovely of you to have us just the same as ever," Madam greeted Mrs. Davenport sincerely and cordially, "just lovely! It's the true Christmas spirit. You don't know how we all appreciate it."

Cordelia Davenport smiled vaguely. Was this sarcasm? She remembered uncomfortably the costly present she had received from Madam a year ago.

"Yes?" she parried pleasantly.

"And the invitations are too delightful. So informal. I told Sis I hoped she would always come hereafter to deliver them—she is growing into a very charming young lady."

"Yes," Cordelia assented, "I'm very proud of my girl—she is so trustworthy."

What had Sis done? What had happened? But Sis *was* trustworthy. Mrs. Davenport said it over frantically to herself while she smiled at her guest.

"We are all so delighted with your idea of entertaining us simply. It is so different!"

Madam Ludington's good faith was evident, but Cordelia could scarcely appreciate it—she was too much alarmed.

"I think," she said with sudden inspiration, and she

marveled at herself as she said it, "that a merry Christmas is not dependent on a bank account."

The plump, shrewd face of her neighbor lighted suddenly. "But we had forgotten that!" she exclaimed.

When James Sr. came home for dinner, he was unusually jovial. His wife told him of Madam Ludington's visit.

"Trust the Davenports for upholding the family honor"—he laughed easily—"they've never failed yet, and they never will. James Jr. and Sis came into the office this afternoon and told me they were going to entertain the usual crowd on five dollars. What do you think of that? Sis said she would bake four dozen cookies after some recipe she learned at school."

Cordelia stared.

"Four dozen cookies!" she cried. "They aren't expecting to feed Madam Ludington and the rest on *cookies?*"

James Sr. looked alarmed. This appalling deduction had not occurred to him. But relief at the attitude of his son and daughter had made him feel lighthearted.

"Well, perhaps that isn't enough," he returned quickly. "Madam is a hearty eater." Then they both laughed till they cried.

"It will be perfectly awful," she sobbed, "to give those people cookies, but the children mean well!"

Then she dried her eyes and went to arrange her hair. But she stopped short in astonishment.

"James!" she called. "James, come here!"

Before them, where the long broad mirror had hung, was a plain bare wall, and near the center, in an inadequate attempt to fill the space, hung James Sr.'s shaving glass. Stuck to the wall with a pin was a bit of paper scrawled in the handwriting of Jim Jr. MERRY CHRISTMAS, FOLKS! it challenged. They were disarmed. There was nothing to do but laugh and wonder. The little paper as much as said: "Don't ask any questions."

James Sr. was silent for a space.

"Cordelia," he said finally, "we've grown away—far away from the old simple good times. Perhaps the children can bring us back. Let's not worry about their plans. We can trust them. Let's be game."

Mrs. Davenport gazed at him contemplatively, a slight smile beginning to curl about the corners of her mouth.

"Why"—she hesitated—"why, perhaps you're right."

That night, when James Sr. came downstairs to dinner, he tripped on an innocent-looking yellow bag that stood on the lower step. By an agile leap he saved his life and landed on the rug while a little stream of lemons rolled gaily across the polished floor.

"Uh-oh!" muttered Jim Jr. to Sis in the dining room. "I forgot to take away that bag."

A new faction had arisen at Cedar Hill, eager, inventive, at work for the preservation of a nearly lost holiday. All that merry Christmas had meant, all that it had failed to mean because of worldliness and social bickerings, hovered fantastically before the residents of Cedar Hill. Secrecy met them at every turn. As the days passed by, the atmosphere became charged to its utmost with a current of mystery such as merry Christmas had not brought for years.

On Christmas Eve there was a final rendezvous in the Davenport drawing room—a flurried, joyous bunch of fourteen Cedar Hill young folks, whom James and Sis had pressed into service for the occasion.

They ranged in age from the youngest Ludington—a five-year-old mannie in curls and kilts—to the Lee twins, just of age and decked in swallowtails and white shirtfronts. James Jr. who had passed his twentieth birthday and overtopped the Lees by two inches, was master of ceremonies, and led proceedings in his gravely dignified way. Next to him was Isabelle Clyde, the tall blonde, beautiful in blue chiffon, and then Sis—black-crowned Sis, whose graceful ways and glorious blue-black hair were attractions that made one forget the color of her gown.

Hastily they stationed themselves in the front hall,

the Lee twins, butler-wise at either side of the drawing room entrance ready to pull the curtains; James Jr. and Sis waiting to receive, and the rest hustling to the place allotted to them, to tune their various instruments. There was indeed an orchestra. It consisted of one piano, one violin, four ukuleles, and three combs, well papered, well tuned.

What a travesty on the usual Davenport recital! Will the proud Cedar Hillites be game? Is the contrast too great? Is it indeed true that it does not rain Christmas festivities— that we must buy them? At this moment Sis turned an appealing glance toward James Jr. Did he, too, feel the inadequacy of their attempt? But her brother's eyes were fixed toward the top of the carved oak staircase where his mother and father were descending, evidently determined to be game whatever the cost, and smilingly concealing any misgivings.

As they reached the hall below, Cordelia glanced at the floor. The rugs were gone, and from the big front door stretched a strip of canvas, fastened carefully with thumbtacks.

"What's this for?" she asked in surprise, turning to her son.

"We don't know, Mother," James Jr. told her with a grin. "Mr. Lee asked us to put it down."

"Mr. Lee!"

At that instant sounded a lugubrious thud on the front porch, followed by shouts of laughter. The door burst open, and in rushed Mr. Lee, Mr. Ludington, Mr. Clyde, and all the other guests, dragging a heavy weight across the mysterious canvas.

"Hello, Davenport! Got a place for this thing?"

"Oh, oh, a Yule log! All decorated with holly—how perfectly lovely! Wait, I'll help!"

Pushing and laughing, the orchestra piled into the hall to see.

"It ought to have come at sundown," explained Clyde, "but the invitation said eight o'clock, so—" He gave a final heave, and the huge thing settled into place, and the festive fire was lighted.

Never had the Davenport Christmas entertainment started in so unceremonious a fashion. The company stood about, talking excitedly, and not till the old Yule log was actually beginning to kindle did they go upstairs to remove their wraps.

Cordelia turned to Sis and James Jr. "It's going to be perfectly splendid!" she said under her breath. "Your father and I almost worried, but they are taking it beautifully."

The music had begun—the violin wailed, the combs buzzed. Sis seized her mother's arm and pointed. Cordelia Davenport gasped. Down the staircase came Mr. and Mrs. Lee, arm in arm in solemnity unequaled, and behind them trooped the other guests, all arrayed in costumes the splendor of which no Davenport recital had ever witnessed. Mrs. Lee's gown was composed completely of ruffles from the Sunday comic section, in pink and red and blue. Her husband was in black and white, as became a gentleman, with narrow spiral ruffles of the *Daily Tribune* and the *Argus-Herald* encasing each leg and arm.

Were they game? Could anything in all the great town, with its wealth and pride, its poverty and greater pride, its struggles and sorrows, its jealousies and joys, equal the true Christmas spirit of haughty Grandmother Ludington in her rustling gown of fine-print want ads?

The youngest Ludington jumped before her and clapped his hands and cried, "Oh, Gamma! Gamma!" and jumped again and lost his balance on the waxed floor, and had to be hugged and comforted.

The orchestra trembled and squeaked, and failed in laughter. The guests rustled and swished and laughed, while the

Lee twins, faithful to their office, drew back the heavy crimson portieres and revealed the Christmas drawing room. There were no festoons of ground pine, no holly wreaths, not even the ancient bunch of mistletoe—but a blaze of glory that dazzled and blinded. The walls were lined with plate-glass mirrors, full-length, expansive, reflecting and reflecting in bewildering infinity, multiplying a thousandfold the candles burning in Cordelia Davenport's cut-glass candlesticks. There was the big library mirror with its gilded frame, the mirrors from dining room, hall, and guest rooms, and all the family looking glasses—everything that would reflect. And in the center of the room, upon a tiny table, stood a diminutive Davenport Christmas tree, its tiny candles glittering and winking at their million reproductions reflected on every side. There were fifty Christmas trees—there were hundreds—thousands, it seemed! There were twenty-five guests—there were fifty—there were one hundred!

And then the recital began with an opening chorus by the Cedar Hill, Jr., fourteen—a quaint old Christmas carol they had learned at school.

After the singing was over, Ludington turned to James Sr.

"This is great!" he cried. "Why didn't we ever do it

before? What's this, Sis? Going to give these to me?" he went on comically. She had paused before him with a silver tray of tiny cards.

Sis laughed. "No, sir. You may have just one. We're going to set you all to work. The card will tell you what to do."

"Number four! Number four! Where's number four?" called Archie Clyde, rushing frantically about.

"Oh, Isabelle, are you seven? You and I are to beat the eggs!"

"Number four—number four!"

James Sr. roused. "What's all this about? Why, I'm number four—my card is marked 'Four.' Here, Archie, what do you want?"

The boy poised on one leg in front of him, and read from his card; " 'Help number four turn the freezers.' "

" 'When the gong sounds, lead the way to the kitchen,' " read Mrs. Lee meditatively. "Why, where *is* the kitchen?"

Madam Ludington was adjusting her eyeglasses. "Here, somebody," she cried. "Do read my card for me!" She handed it to a curly-headed Ludington.

"Oh, Grandma! You are to cut the cake! Oh, isn't this fun? Wait—I'll tell you what it says. 'Please cut the cake, which you will find on the broad shelf in the serving room.

There is a knife in the left-hand upper drawer of the kitchen cabinet.' "

"Oh," cried Madam, "how can I ever do anything in these paper furbelows?"

A gong sounded above the din. "Come on, everybody," called Mrs. Lee. "We're going to the kitchen!"

"The freezers are all packed. All you have to do is keep them rolling," explained James Sr. to Archie, after an examination of the two rounded tubs, which seemed screwed to the table.

"Where's the eggbeater? Where's the——"

"Doesn't it tell? Why, yes! 'On hanger above the sink.' Here it is!"

Such laughter, such informality, never had been known. The newspapered guests flew back and forth. They folded paper napkins, they arranged plates of cookies, they beat eggs, and turned them stiff and foaming into the lemon sherbet. They carried chairs, they drew water and filled glasses.

"I'm to light the candles on the cake," sang Mrs. Clyde, "but where are the matches?"

"Here—here—in this tin box!"

At last all was ready, and the company returned to the Christmas drawing room to eat what they themselves had served.

"You see, we couldn't have a caterer," Sis explained.

"Ladies and gentlemen!" the voice of James Jr. rose above the din, and they looked to where he stood, straight and tall, between the bay windows. "Ladies and gentlemen. Twenty-five years ago tonight, on Cedar Hill, in the Davenport parlor, nine persons gathered to celebrate Christmas Eve. On that night a compact was made in the light of the Christmas candles to the effect that so long as they were neighbors, in sickness, or in health, in adversity as well as prosperity, they would, unless unavoidably prevented, spend each ensuing Christmas night together.

Those nine persons were Mr. and Mrs. Frank Clyde, Mr. and Mrs. Walter Lee, Mr. and Mrs. Eugene Ludington, Madam Ludington, and Mr. and Mrs. James Davenport.

"Wherefore we, the children and heirs of the aforesaid persons, have determined that, so long as the power within us lies, we will, with sincerity and goodwill to all, aid and abet the aforesaid persons, and if at any time their courage fails, or money is otherwise diverted, we will, by reason of our inherited ability and traditional inventiveness, provide such entertainment as may be needed for the annual occasion.

"In token whereof we present you with this birthday cake, holding twenty-five candles, each one of which represents a single Christmas celebration during the past quarter century. And," he added with a grin, "as there are now twenty-five of us, including two guests, there is just one piece apiece, with a candle for each!"

Cordelia Davenport's eyes glowed. She turned to her daughter.

"Oh, Sis!" she breathed. "How did you know? Who told you?"

"Madam Ludington. And oh, Mother, she's been just the best help! She suggested the paper costumes, too. Do look at her!"

The old lady was shaking with laughter while she tried to repair a damaged paper flounce with pins.

And then, at last, amid the clamor of tongues there sounded distant sweet chords. Intrigued, the guests sought the source. In the music room the youngest Ludington, the little mannie in curls and kilts, stood by the grand piano looking at Sis. All the lanterns and candles but one had been extinguished. There was a sudden hush.

Sis played the opening chord of Martin Luther's beloved children's hymn, the child turned and began to sing:

Away in a manger, no crib for a bed,
The little Lord Jesus laid down His sweet head.

The stars in the bright sky looked down where He lay,
The little Lord Jesus asleep on the hay!

Across the room where the singer gazed as he sang was a crèche, illuminated by three candles. As the last notes died away into the night, there followed absolute silence.

Christ had returned to Cedar Hill Christmas.

The Tiny Foot

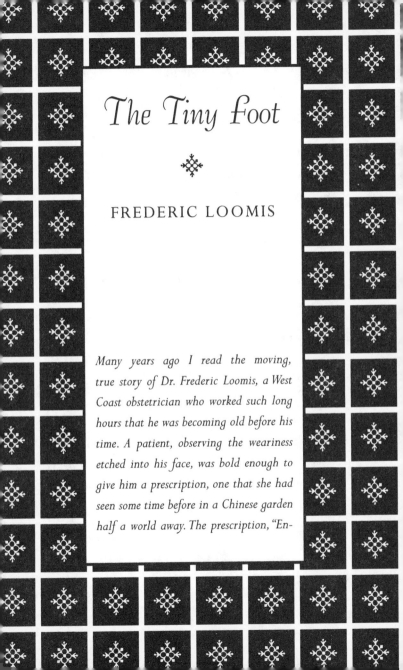

❄

FREDERIC LOOMIS

Many years ago I read the moving, true story of Dr. Frederic Loomis, a West Coast obstetrician who worked such long hours that he was becoming old before his time. A patient, observing the weariness etched into his face, was bold enough to give him a prescription, one that she had seen some time before in a Chinese garden half a world away. The prescription, "En-

joy yourself; it's later than you think," radically altered Dr. Loomis's life.

And so when, six years later, I came across another story having to do with Dr. Loomis, I read it with more than ordinary interest. I have never been able to get this story, "The Tiny Foot," out of my mind. Short as it was, there was no question but that it had to be included in this collection.

I don't believe it was mere happenstance that I subsequently stumbled on Consultation Room in an old bookstore, hemmed in by tens of thousands of paperback books. It was written by my old friend Dr. Loomis. Imagine my surprise and delight to discover that one chapter of the book tells in full the larger story of the tiny foot. Thus the inclusion of the fuller story in the Christmas in My Heart series represents, I believe, the first time the full story has been included in a Christmas collection. Since Dr. James Dobson used it as the Focus on the Family Christmas story of the year in 1993, millions have fallen in love with it.

The story has to do with a terrible decision Dr. Loomis was once forced to make: whether to enable a deformed fetus to be born. (Remember, however, that this story took place before cesarean operations radically changed medical history.) I strongly suspect that you will not be able to forget the story, either.

"Doctor, just a moment, please, before you go into the delivery room."

The man was about thirty-five, well dressed and intelligent, an executive of a large oil company. His first baby was to arrive within the hour. He had spent the preceding hours by his wife's bedside, miserable with the feeling of helplessness and anxiety common to all prospective fathers at such a time, but nevertheless standing by to comfort her by his presence.

"I must tell you one thing before the baby gets here, Doctor," he said. "I want that baby and so does Irene, more than we ever wanted anything else, I think—but *not* if it isn't all right. I want you to promise me right now that if it is defective—and I know you can usually tell—you will not let it live. No one need ever know it, but *it must not live*. I am depending on you."

Few doctors have escaped that problem. I had not been in California long before I encountered it there, just as I had encountered it elsewhere. Fortunately, it is a problem that usually solves itself. Babies that are defective, either mentally or physically, after all are infrequent. Yet the possibility of having one hounds almost every waiting mother. Her first question on opening her eyes after a baby is born is always either "What is it?" or "Is it all right?" Whichever question comes first, the other invariably follows, and the one as to its condition is always the more important.

However they may feel about it in individual instances, doctors rightly resent and resist the rather persistent effort to make them the judges of life and death. Our load of responsibility is enough without that. "Judgment is difficult," Hippocrates said, "when the preservation of life is the only question." If the added burden of deciding whether or not life *should* be preserved were placed upon us, it would be entirely too much. Moreover, the entire morale of medicine would be immediately threatened or destroyed.

Two years after I came to California, there came to my office one day a fragile young woman, expecting her first baby. Her history was not good from an emotional standpoint, though she came from a fine family.

I built her up as well as I could and found her increasingly wholesome and interesting as time went on, partly because of the effort she was making to be calm and patient and to keep her emotional and nervous reactions under control.

One month before her baby was due, her routine examination showed that her baby was in a breech position.

As a rule, the baby's head is in the lower part of the uterus for months before delivery, not because it is heavier and "sinks" in the surrounding fluid, but simply because it fits more comfortably in that position. There is no routine spontaneous "turning" of all babies at the seventh or eighth month, as is so generally supposed, but the occasional baby found in a breech position in the last month not infrequently changes to the normal vertex position with the head down by the time it is ready to be born, so that only about one baby in twenty-five is born in the breech position.

This is fortunate, as the death rate of breech babies is comparatively high because of the difficulty in delivering the after-coming head, and the imperative need of delivering it rather quickly after the body is born. At that moment the cord becomes compressed between the baby's hard little head and the mother's bony pelvis. When no oxygen reaches the baby's bloodstream, it inevitably dies in a few short minutes. Everyone in the delivery room is tense, except the mother herself, in a breech delivery, especially if it is a first baby, when the difficulty is greater. The mother is usually quietly asleep or almost so.

The case I was speaking of was a "complete" breech—the baby's legs and feet being folded under it, tailor-fashion—in contrast to the "frank" breech, in which the thighs and legs are folded back on a baby's body like a jackknife, the little rear end backing its way into the world first of all.

The hardest thing for the attending doctor to do with any breech delivery is to keep his hands away from it until the natural forces of expulsion have thoroughly dilated the firm maternal structures that delay its progress. I waited as patiently as I could, sending frequent messages to the excited family in the corridor outside.

At last the time had come, and I gently drew down one little foot. I grasped the other but, for some reason I could not understand, it would not come down beside the first one. I pulled again, gently enough but with a little force, with light pressure on the abdomen from above by my assisting nurse, and the baby's body moved down just enough for me to see that it was a little girl—and then, to my consternation, I saw that the other foot would *never* be beside the first one. The entire thigh from the hip to the knee was missing and that one foot never could reach below the opposite knee. And a baby girl was to suffer this, a curious defect that I had never seen before, nor have I since!

There followed the hardest struggle I have ever had with myself. I knew what a dreadful effect it would have upon the unstable nervous system of the mother. I felt sure that the family would almost certainly impoverish itself in taking the child to every famous orthopedist in the world whose achievements might offer a ray of hope.

Most of all, I saw this little girl sitting sadly by herself while other girls laughed and danced and ran and played—and then I suddenly realized that there was something that would save every pang but one, and that one thing was in my power.

One breech baby in ten dies in delivery because it is not delivered rapidly enough, and now—if only I did not hurry! If I could slow my hand, if I could make myself delay those few short moments. It would not be an easy delivery, anyway. No one in all this world would ever know. The mother, after the first shock of grief, would probably be glad she had lost a child so sadly handicapped. In a year or two she would try again and this tragic fate would never be repeated.

"Don't bring this suffering upon them," the small voice within me said. "This baby has never taken a breath—don't let her ever take one. You probably can't get it out in time, anyway. *Don't hurry.* Don't be a fool and bring this terrible thing upon them. Suppose your conscience does hurt a little; can't you stand it better than they can? Maybe your conscience will hurt worse if you *do* get it out in time."

I motioned to the nurse for the warm sterile towel that is always ready for me in a breech delivery to wrap around the baby's body so that the stimulation of the cold air of the outside world may not induce a sudden expansion of the baby's chest, causing the aspiration of fluid or mucus that might bring death.

But this time the towel was only to conceal from the attending nurses that which my eyes alone had seen. With the touch of that pitiful little foot in my hand, a pang of sorrow for the baby's future swept through me, and my decision was made.

I glanced at the clock. Three of the allotted seven or eight minutes had already gone. Every eye in the room was upon me and I could feel the tension in their eagerness to do instantly what I asked, totally unaware of what I was feeling. I hoped they could not possibly detect the tension of my own struggle at that moment.

These nurses had seen me deliver dozens of breech babies successfully—yes, and they had seen me fail, too. Now they were going to see me fail again. For the first time in my medical life I was deliberately discarding what I had been taught was right for something that I felt sure was better.

I slipped my hand beneath the towel to feel the pulsations of the baby's cord, a certain index of its condition. Two or three minutes more would be enough. So that I might seem to be doing something, I drew the baby down a little lower to "split out" the arms, the usual next step, and as I did so the little pink foot on the good side bobbed out from its protecting towel and pressed firmly against my slowly moving hand, the hand into whose keeping the safety of the mother and the baby had been entrusted. There was a sudden convulsive movement of the baby's body, an actual feeling of strength and life and vigor.

It was too much. I couldn't do it. I delivered the baby with her pitiful little leg. I told the family and the next day, with a catch in my voice, I told the mother.

Every foreboding came true. The mother was in a hospital for several months. I saw her once or twice and she looked like a wraith of her former self. I heard of them indirectly from time to time. They had been to Rochester, Minnesota. They had been to Chicago and to Boston. Finally I lost track of them altogether.

As the years went on, I blamed myself bitterly for not having had the strength to yield to my temptation.

Through the many years that I have been here, there has developed in our hospital a pretty custom of staging an elaborate Christmas party each year for the employees, the nurses, and the doctors of the staff.

There is always a beautifully decorated tree on the

stage of our little auditorium. The girls spend weeks in preparation. We have so many difficult things to do during the year, so much discipline, and so many of the stern realities of life, that we have set aside this one day to touch upon the emotional and spiritual side. It is almost like going to an impressive church service, as each year we dedicate ourselves anew to the year ahead.

This past year the arrangement was somewhat changed. The tree, on one side of the stage, had been sprayed with silver paint and was hung with scores of gleaming silver and tinsel ornaments, without a trace of color anywhere and with no lights hung upon the tree itself. It shown but faintly in the dimly lighted auditorium.

Every doctor of the staff who could possibly be there was in his seat. The first rows were reserved for the nurses and in a moment the procession entered, each girl in uniform, each one crowned by her nurse's cap, her badge of office. Around their shoulders were their blue Red Cross capes, one end tossed back to show the deep red lining.

We rose as one man to do them honor, and as the last one reached her seat and we settled in our places again, the organ began the opening notes of one of the oldest of our carols.

Slowly down the middle aisle, marching from the back of the auditorium, came twenty other girls singing softly, our own nurses, in full uniform, each holding high a lighted candle, while through the auditorium floated the familiar strains of "Silent Night." We were on our feet again instantly. I could have killed anyone who spoke to me then, because I couldn't have answered, and by the time they reached their seats I couldn't see.

And then a great blue floodlight at the back was turned on very slowly, gradually covering the tree with increasing splendor: brighter and brighter, until every ornament was almost a flame. On the opposite side of the stage a curtain was slowly drawn and we saw three lovely young musicians, all in shimmering white evening gowns. They played very softly in unison with the organ—a harp, a cello, and a violin. I am quite sure I was not the only old sissy there whose eyes were filled with tears.

I have always liked the harp and I love to watch the grace of a skillful player. I was especially fascinated by this young harpist. She played extraordinarily well, as if she loved it. Her slender fingers flickered across the strings, and as the nurses sang, her face, made beautiful by a mass of auburn hair, was upturned as if the world that moment were a wonderful and holy place.

I waited, when the short program was over, to congratulate the chief nurse on the unusual effects she had arranged. And as I sat alone, there came running down the aisle a woman whom I did not know. She came to me with arms outstretched.

"Oh, you *saw* her," she cried. "You must have recognized your baby. That was my daughter who played the harp—and I saw you watching her. Don't you remember the little girl who was born with only one good leg seventeen years ago? We tried everything else first, but now she has a whole artificial leg on that side—but you would never know it, would you? She can walk, she can swim, and she can almost dance.

"But, best of all, through all those years when she couldn't do those things, she learned to use her hands so wonderfully. She is going to be one of the world's great harpists. She enters the university this year at seventeen. She is my whole life and now she is so happy. . . . And here she is!"

As we spoke, this sweet young girl had quietly approached us, her eyes glowing, and now she stood beside me.

"This is your first doctor, my dear—our doctor," her mother said. Her voice trembled. I could see her literally swept back, as I was, through all the years of heartache to the day when I told her what she had to face. "He was the first one to tell me about you. He brought you to me."

Impulsively I took the child in my arms. Across her

118

warm young shoulder I saw the creeping clock of the delivery room of seventeen years before. I lived again those awful moments when her life was in my hand, when I had decided on deliberate infanticide.

I held her away from me and looked at her.

"You never will know, my dear," I said, "you never will know, nor will anyone else in all the world, just what tonight has meant to me. Go back to your harp for a moment, please—and play 'Silent Night' for me alone. I have a load on my shoulders that no one has ever seen, a load that only you can take away."

Her mother sat beside me and quietly took my hand as her daughter played. Perhaps she knew what was in my mind. And as the last strains of "Silent Night, Holy Night" faded again, I think I found the answer, and the comfort, I had waited for so long.

A Christmas Ballad for the Captain

✳

WILLIAM J. LEDERER

There is something about war that brings out the unvarnished person that is so often hidden by peacetime glaze. But even in war, one's true colors are often concealed, for a time at least, from those one daily interacts with.

So many of us, in peace or war, classify people as being "good" or "bad"; sometimes we are right, and sometimes we are not. With reference to the "Old Man" and the "Unholy K's," perceptions proved to be something less than reliable.

William J. Lederer, author of such World War II classics as **All the Ships at Sea** and **Ensign O'Toole and Me**; and coauthor of **The Ugly American**, remembers a wartime Christmas that was like no other. It was early in the war, and Lederer was an officer on a Navy destroyer. On the return home from the terrible Battle of Anzio, the ship was torpedoed. Lederer wrote down this true story as a Christmas memory of the ship's crew and captain, and then sent copies to those sailors who survived.

It was picked up by the popular press and quickly became one of the most beloved stories of the war. Reader's Digest editors featured it as their 1960 Christmas issue story; more recently, it anchored Lederer's **A Happy Book of Christmas Stories**, published by W. W. Norton in 1981, and it was featured in the 1993 Family Circle Christmas Treasury.

Mr. Lederer is still writing from his beloved Vermont. He is a fascinating gentleman, both to talk with and to hear from by letter. Especially when he talks about the many literary luminaries he has known through the years. He concurs with Hemingway, whom he knew well, that an author who lacks kindness will never be able to write stories that are worth reading.

Captain Elias Stark, commanding officer of our destroyer, was a square-shouldered New Hampshire man, as quiet and austere as the granite mountains of his native state. About the only time the enlisted men heard him talk was when they first reported aboard. He would invite them to his cabin for a one-minute speech of welcome, then question them about their families, and note the names and addresses of the sailors' next of kin.

That was the way he had first met the "Unholy K's"— Krakow, Kratch, Koenig, and Kelly. They had arrived with a draft of seventeen men from the naval prison at Portsmouth, New Hampshire. Most of the prison group were bad eggs, but the worst were these four sailors from a small coal-mining town in Pennsylvania. They had chests and shoulders like buffaloes, fists like sledgehammers, black stubble beards, and manners to match.

They had once been good kids, the mainstays of St. Stephen's choir in their hometown, but somehow they had gone astray. They seemed to specialize in getting into trouble together, as a quartet. All four went into the Navy direct from reform school. Within six months they were in serious trouble again and had been sent to Portsmouth Naval Prison.

When they were called to the captain's cabin, they listened to his speech with exaggerated expressions of boredom. Then the Old Man broke out his record book to note the names and addresses of their next of kin. He looked up inquiringly.

Krakow, the leader of the Unholy K's, took the initiative. Spreading his tremendous arms, he pulled Kelly, Kratch, and Koenig into a tight circle. "The four of us, sir, ain't got no family. We ain't got parents or wives or relatives." He paused. "All we got is girlfriends, eh, fellas?"

Captain Stark simply puffed on his pipe. Patiently he asked, "Would you give me your best ladies' names and addresses for our records?"

The Unholy K's glanced at one another.

Krakow said, "Sir, we don't feel like it's an officer's business who our girls are." He stopped as Kelly tugged his sleeve and whispered to him.

"Okay," continued Krakow sarcastically, "you want to know who our best girls are, I'll tell you. Mine's Rita Hayworth, Kelly's is Ginger Rogers, Kratch's is Lana Turner, and Koenig's is Paulette Goddard. They all got the same address: Hollywood, sir."

"Very well," said the captain, "I will list those names in my records. Thank you, that will be all."

As soon as the Unholy K's got below deck they began bragging how they had made a fool out of the Old Man. Kelly started a bawdy song, and Krakow, Kratch, and Koenig joined in. Each man, in turn, made up a lyric while the other three harmonized. They had splendid voices, and with their choirboy training they formed a wonderful quartet. They sang four unprintable verses about the captain and why he wanted their girls' addresses.

Actually, the captain had a good reason for obtaining personal information about the men. He strongly believed it was his duty to keep their families informed on how they were getting along. So, once every three months, in blunt New England fashion, he sent a personal note written in a tiny, neat hand to everyone's next of kin.

For example:

Dear Madam,

Your son John is well—and is happy as can be expected in North Atlantic gales. If he shaved more often and cleaned his clothes more meticulously he would be more popular with his division chief.

I think highly of him as a gunner's mate and, with luck, you should see him in a few months. You will find he has put on twelve pounds, and the extra flesh hangs well on him.

Sincerely,
Elias Stark
Commander, U.S. Navy

In September, after a year in the combat zone, our destroyer went to the Brooklyn Navy Yard for a three-week overhaul. Almost all the officers and men went home on furloughs. Only the Old Man stayed on board the entire time, working alone, day and night. No one knew the nature of his apparently urgent business; but whenever we passed his cabin we saw him hunched over his desk, scratching away with an old-fashioned pen, while his cherrywood pipe sent up clouds of blue smoke.

We were puzzled also by the scores of parcels in plain wrappers that began coming to the Old Man before we sailed. It was not until much later that we would find out what they contained.

Meanwhile, our destroyer had gone to sea again, protecting convoys across the North Atlantic to England. It was rough work. Icy gales battered us; ships were torpedoed almost every night. We had little sleep and much physical discomfort. Everyone drooped with fatigue. Tempers became edgy, and there were fights. Captain Stark was constantly on the bridge, smoking his pipe and watching everything carefully. Despite the fact that his clear blue eyes became bloodshot from exhaustion and he stooped a bit from weariness, he remained calm and aloof.

If he knew how the Unholy K's were trying to destroy the ship's morale, he never mentioned it. It was their well-rendered ballads that did the dirty work. Everyone was afraid of these four bullies; but when they sang insidious songs about the ship's officers, the crew listened. Their lyrics were so catchy that a song rendered in the aftercrew's washroom would be repeated all over the ship within a half hour. No officers ever heard the four men sing; but the results of their music were uncomfortably apparent.

The Unholy K's had one song about the hundreds of packages the captain had locked in the forward peak tank. The lyrics said that the boxes contained silk stockings, cigarettes, whiskey, drugs, and other black-market goods the captain was going to sell in England. They depicted the captain becoming a millionaire and retiring to a mansion in New Hampshire as soon as the war was over.

The crew began to ask questions: Why *should* the Old Man be hiding the parcels? Why *had* they been delivered with so much secrecy? It was even rumored that the Old Man was head of a black-market cartel and the cartons contained drugs stolen from Navy supply depots. But when the crew saw Captain Stark, tall, quiet, dignified, they knew in their hearts that the rumors were impossible.

In mid-December we shoved off from Newfoundland with another convoy. There were sixty-two ships in the group, many of them tankers filled with high-octane aviation gas. Almost immediately we ran into a gale. The ships wallowed and floundered among mountainous waves. For nearly a week we had nothing to eat but sandwiches, and it was impossible to sleep. On top of this misery, we received an emergency alert and intelligence that the largest Nazi submarine wolf pack ever assembled was shadowing our convoy.

After a few days at sea, all grumbling and grousing stopped. We were too weary to do anything but stand watch, straining our eyes and ears for the enemy. Finally the storm slackened and the submarines closed in. During the beginning of the second week, hardly a night went by without the sky lighting up with the explosions of torpedoed ships.

Then, at sunrise on the twenty-fifth of December, as we neared the southwest tip of Ireland, our protection arrived—Royal Navy planes. The seas calmed and we relaxed; for the first time in what had seemed ages, the men were able to get a hot meal and sleep. All hands, except those on watch, turned in thankfully, exhausted.

Suddenly at nine o'clock on this Christmas morning, the bosun's mate piped reveille. A wave of grumbling passed over the ship. We had all expected to be able to sleep in unless there was an attack. A few minutes later, Captain Stark's voice came over the loudspeaker. "This is the captain speaking. Shipmates, I know you are tired and want to sleep. But today is Christmas. There are special surprise packages from your families. They have been unloaded from the forward peak tanks and have been distributed throughout the ship alphabetically."

The news exploded through the ship. Men scrambled for their packages. Sailors sat all over the decks, cutting string, tearing paper, wiping away tears, and shouting to shipmates about what they had received.

But the four Unholy K's found no presents. They stood together, watching the others sullenly.

"Christmas!" said Koenig. "It's only an excuse to get suckers to spend money."

"Don't show *me* your new wristwatch," sneered Krakow to a young sailor who proudly held it up. "If I need a new ticker, I'll buy me one."

One happy kid came jigging up with a huge box of

fudge. "From my girl," he sang out. "Now I see why the Old Man wanted her name and address."

"Hey!" said Krakow, grabbing Kelly's arm. "Didn't we give the Old Man *our* girls' names and addresses?"

"Yeah," said Kratch, beginning to grin slyly. "Rita Hayworth, Ginger Rogers, Lana Turner, and Paulette Goddard."

"Then how come we didn't get anything?"

"Let's go see the Old Man."

The Unholy K's, smiling evilly, went to the captain's cabin.

"Captain Stark, sir," said Krakow with mock respect, "we got a complaint. Everybody on this ship got presents from the names and addresses they gave you."

The captain looked at the four men gravely. "Don't you think that's pretty nice?"

"But we gave you names and addresses, and we didn't get no presents."

"Oh, you didn't?" said the Old Man slowly.

"No, sir, everyone but us. That's discrimination, sir."

"By gum," said the captain, standing up, "there *are* four extra packages. Now I just wonder . . ." He went to his bunk and pulled a blanket off a pile of parcels.

"There's one for me!" hollered Kelly, surging forward.

Captain Stark stood up to his full six feet and blocked

130

the way. Reaching into the bunk, he handed out the packages to the four men, one at a time.

"Now, if you'll excuse me, I'll conduct Yuletide services for all hands." He went out to the bridge.

The Unholy K's ripped the colored wrappings. Krakow couldn't open his fast enough and took his sheath knife to slash the ribbon. Inside the fancy box was a pair of knitted woolen gloves. He tried them on his big red hands.

"Gee, the right size!"

There was something else in the box. It was a picture of a shapely woman in a low-cut dress; and there was writing on it.

> Dear Joe Krakow,
>
> I knitted these gloves especially for you because you are my best boyfriend in the U.S. Navy. I hope that they'll keep you warm and that you'll have a wonderful Christmas wherever you may be.
>
> From your best gal,
> Rita Hayworth

Joe Krakow felt around his pockets for a handkerchief but couldn't find one. "What did you guys get?" he said, sniffling.

"Me?" said Koenig shrilly. "I got a wallet and a picture of Paulette Goddard! *From Paulette Goddard!*"

Kelly received a watch and an autographed picture from Ginger Rogers; and Kratch's present from Lana Turner was a gold fountain pen and a sentimentally inscribed photograph.

The Unholy K's shuffled around to the bridge where Captain Stark, his Bible open, stood in front of the microphone.

Krakow said, "Captain, sir . . ."

"Later," the captain replied bluntly, without even turning. He switched on the loudspeaker, announced church services, and read the story of the Nativity to all hands. Below, in the engine room, men listened, and in the chiefs' quarters, in the galley, in the mess compartments—throughout the ship, 250 sailors listened as the Old Man read the story of Jesus.

When he finished, he said he hoped everyone would join him in singing a few carols.

The Unholy K's pushed in on the captain. "Let us help you, sir," said Krakow urgently.

"This is not your type of song," the captain replied.

"Please, sir, the least we can do is lead the singing."

"Please, sir, let this be *our* Christmas present to *you.*"

"A Christmas present for me?" mused the Old Man.

132

"Why, yes, we'd all appreciate having a choir for the occasion. What shall we start with?"

The four sailors looked at the Old Man and then down at the photographs and presents clutched tightly under their arms. They gathered around the microphone. Krakow coughed; then in his deep bass he boomed, "Shipmates, this is Koenig, Kelly, Kratch, and me, Krakow—four no-good bums. Today is Christmas, and we want to sing you a special ballad." He paused, and wiped his eyes and nose on his shirtsleeve.

Krakow raised his hand like a symphony conductor, and the quartet began to sing:

Silent night, holy night,
All is calm, all is bright . . .

The magic of the holy music spread. Everyone on the ship joined in. The helmsman and the officer of the deck put their throats to the Christmas ballad. Even Captain Elias Stark, the granite man from New Hampshire, moved into the quartet, inclined his head, and, in reedy tenor, swelled the song.

Sleep in heavenly peace,
Sleep in heavenly peace.

The joyous music rose above the noise of the ocean and the destroyer's engines. During the third stanza an enormous bird soared in from the low-hanging clouds and landed in the after rigging. It flapped its great wings and made noises as if it, too, were singing our Christmas ballad along with us. My shipmates said it was an albatross. But, even though my eyes were filled with tears, I'd swear that it was an angel.

Of course, that was many years ago when I was still a kid. But even then I could recognize an angel when I saw one. As sure as my name's Joe Krakow.

Jolly Miss Enderby

❄

PAUL GALLICO

Why is it that being overweight is equated with being jolly? How often might a smiling face hide a crying heart? Why don't we take the time to look behind the façade and search out the person behind?

"Jolly" Miss Enderby and those who supposedly knew her well were all of the above: yes, she was fat; yes, she was taken for granted; and yes, she was a most lonely

woman . . . but having lost all hope that anyone would ever take the trouble to care.

Paul Gallico (1897–1976), author of bestsellers such as The Poseidon Adventure, The Snow Goose, Thomasina, The Lonely, *and others, often zeroed in on characters who were not what they seemed to be. This is one of his most disturbing—most disturbing because he hits most of us where we are weakest.*

Jolly Miss Enderby! So she was known and spoken of, and who would have denied it seeing her round dimpled face alight with vivacity, her smile spreading to her extra chins, for she was a fat woman, as she sat at the piano in the classroom and played, sang, and conducted all at the same time.

Teacher of the second grade of the Dowsville Elementary School, the occasion was Miss Enderby's annual party and treat. Although the school had closed for the holidays the week before, her party always took place the afternoon of Christmas Eve and the class with parents came back for it. There were recitations, dancing, and singing. Afterward Miss Enderby served little cakes with colored icing

and a choice of either cream soda or root beer. Miss Enderby paid for these herself.

Jolly Miss Enderby with the face of a cherub, her
head, surrounded by an aureole of short-cropped graying
curls, nodding and one fat arm emerging from a flowered
frock giving the tempo of the final carol. She beamed upon
the children, the girls with great bows in their hair, the boys
with scrubbed faces, the elders proud and stiff in their best
clothing. Always cheerful, Miss Enderby made others
cheerful, too.

After that, the refreshments, and the children, urged
by their mothers, shyly handing over their small, badly
wrapped Christmas gifts that soon made a colorful pile
upon Miss Enderby's desk.

One moment the classroom was still alive with the
chattering of the group, congratulations, admonitions to
the children to thank Miss Enderby, and the next it was
empty and silent hard upon the last "Merry Christmas, Miss
Enderby." It had not occurred to any of them to inquire
how she would be spending her Christmas or perhaps to
ask if she might like to join them at their Christmas dinner.
And, of course, it did not occur to Miss Enderby, either,
that anyone should.

The teacher gently let down the lid of the old piano

and went and sat at her desk to review the successful afternoon. The classroom, looking gay with its crisscrossing of scarlet and green crepe paper streamers, the pine branches plucked from the nearby woods, the holly and mistletoe, and its Christmas tree, was full of echoes and silences and things vividly remembered. Well past fifty, unmarried, dedicated, Miss Enderby had been giving these parties for more than twenty years, and there were always endearing little incidents. This time it was Midge Thorgerson's wreath slipping down over her eyes during her solo dance and the Johnson boy forgetting his poem, bursting into tears, running to her, and burying his face in her ample middle.

And the collection of gifts on her desk. Miss Enderby smiled at these. Then the echoes sounded no more, the memories began to fade, and there was only the empty classroom with the lowering winter sun momentarily setting the snow outside afire before it vanished. With all the human bodies no longer there the room was suddenly chilly, and Miss Enderby shivered slightly.

She rose and went about the business of tidying up, depositing the empty paper drinking cups into the big wire basket. She swept the dozen or so presents into her carryall along with a half-finished bottle of cream soda. When she walked down the corridor of the dark and deserted schoolhouse, her heel clicks sounded too loudly in her ears. She donned galoshes and the cloth coat that was never quite warm enough for their winters and went out into the frosty early evening, locking the door behind her.

As she turned homeward there was starshine overhead, and the colored lights of the Christmas trees outside people's houses glowed hospitably. Miss Enderby thought what a good community it was where folks put out Christmas trees so that everyone could enjoy them. She continued on to her lodgings in the boardinghouse of Mrs. Weedon at the far end of Chestnut Street. Mrs. Weedon did not have a Christmas tree on the front lawn.

Miss Enderby's quarters were at the back of the house. The bath was down the hall, but she had a basin in her room with a mirror from which a good deal of the silver backing had departed. She washed, put on lipstick very carefully, reordered her hair, and having completed the task, she said to the visible portion of her mirror image, "There you are, Miss Enderby," and went out again, this time to trudge down the six blocks to Greene's Cafeteria, where she took her meals.

The dingy restaurant had tried to greet Christmas with a few garlands, but it was jolly Miss Enderby who lit up the place when she came in and took her seat at the table in the rear by the kitchen door. The two waitresses, Bella and Madge, and the other patrons were always cheered by her presence.

Her slice of gray Yankee pot roast was concealed under a gluey brown sauce. While Miss Enderby wrestled with it Bella, a thin blonde with untidy hair and a not too clean apron, had a lull and came over.

"Going to the movie tonight? It's Robert Redford and Paul Newman."

Miss Enderby shook her head and said, "No, I'm staying home and opening my presents."

"Presents?" repeated Bella. "Aren't you lucky."

Yes, I am, Miss Enderby thought to herself. Perhaps Bella wouldn't be getting any presents. "But you'll be coming in for the Turkey Dinner Christmas Special tomorrow, won't you? I seen the turkey. They're cooking it now."

"Of course," Miss Enderby replied. When she had finished she rose and said, "Good night, Bella. See you tomorrow."

Bella said with a slight smile of satisfaction, "I'm off tomorrow. Madge will be looking after you. I'm going to my sister's."

Miss Enderby's several chins outlined her pleased smile. "How nice for you, Bella." Miss Enderby had no living relations. But then neither did she have any envy nor self-pity. "Well then, I'll say 'Merry Christmas' now," and leaned over and kissed her.

The two waitresses watched her go out. Madge said to Bella, "Imagine having to eat Christmas dinner alone in a dump like this. It's different when you're working."

"Oh, she don't mind. She's always smiling," Bella replied.

Madge said "Uh-huh" and walked away to a customer. Bella felt vaguely uncomfortable.

Back home in her room as Miss Enderby undid her parcels slowly so as to make them last longer she thought of Bella's words, "Aren't you lucky," and felt that indeed she was, for as the years of teaching came marching past in her mind, this last one could hold up its head, for it had been a good one. Each little packet on the table represented a child, and each child represented too a success or a failure, and there had been more successes than failures.

The first packet contained a cake of soap and its cheap scent suddenly overpowered the staleness of the furnishings of the room. From Kevin Hansen of the angel face and the dark heart; she had broken through to find the affection that also slumbered there. A string of ten-cent store beads. Anna Polanski; she really had improved. A colored washcloth. Mary Cronin, one of her failures; Mary's head was empty. It would remain empty. She comforted herself with thinking, *You can't win them all.*

A self-propelling pencil, a bottle of cheap toilet water, a pincushion, a small badly made China cat, a decorated comb, a hand-embroidered doily, a box of homemade cookies.

The colorful discarded wrapping paper made her room gayer, and the tribute on the table before her filled jolly Miss Enderby's heart with gratitude, and in her mind's eye she saw them all once more as they had been that afternoon in their party clothes and heard again the noise and hubbub as they ate and drank their way through her treat. And then ere she knew it, the picture changed to herself sitting in the empty classroom and the little shiver that had come over her. Before she could prevent it, the shiver repeated itself there in her own room.

Never in a million years would Miss Enderby have admitted to herself that she was suddenly miserable and desperately lonely. She rose and went to the window that looked out upon Mrs. Weedon's untidy backyard. It had begun to snow again and she heard bells from the church. She turned away and suddenly tears began to fall from her eyes. Her stout heart fought against them valiantly. *Oh no no! Never admit that no one cared really.* She sat down at the table and regarded the small gifts, all there would ever be for her Christmas.

There came a timid knock at her door, and it opened slowly to admit Bella from Greene's Cafeteria. She stood there for a moment nonplussed by Miss Enderby's tears.

"Oh," she cried involuntarily, "Madge said you were always smiling."

"I was alone," said Miss Enderby. "There was no one to see me."

"Look," Bella said, "I got a favor to ask. My sister always says I can bring a friend. Christmas is a big party with her. Everyone is there. I . . . I . . . I never had a friend I could ask. Would you come, Miss Enderby, please?"

What healed Miss Enderby's great heart once more, dried her tears, and filled her with a great glow of love was the nobility of the little waitress who could so disguise the invitation, and the teacher's wonderful warm embracing smile broke forth again as she cried, "Oh, Bella, I would love to. What a happy Christmas you will give me!"

Rebecca's Only Way

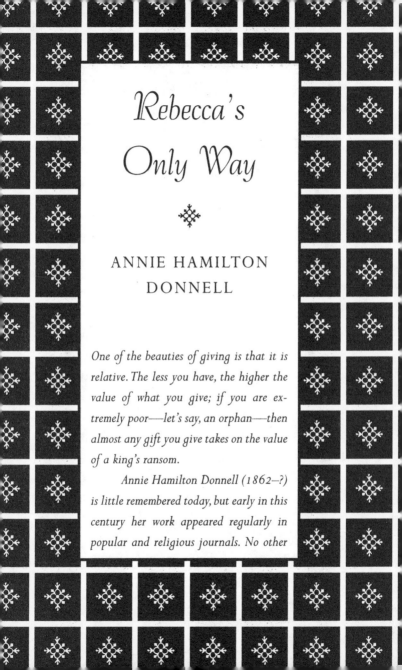

❖

ANNIE HAMILTON DONNELL

One of the beauties of giving is that it is relative. The less you have, the higher the value of what you give; if you are extremely poor—let's say, an orphan—then almost any gift you give takes on the value of a king's ransom.

Annie Hamilton Donnell (1862–?) is little remembered today, but early in this century her work appeared regularly in popular and religious journals. No other

writer I know was more concerned with children who were aban-
doned, rejected, or left alone. This particular story I remember my
mother reciting many times during my childhood. It is safe to say
that no other story Donnell ever wrote has been cherished more
than "Rebecca's Only Way." It is a joy to bring it back from the edge
of extinction and help to give it a new life.

The thin blue line wound evenly through the corridor and
out of the big doors. Just out—no farther. At the first whiff
of the blessed freedom of out-of-doors the line broke into
sixty-three pieces, every "piece" a little free blue orphan.
The silence broke, too, into sixty-three shouts. For an hour
the sixty-three little lone ones would forget that they were
lone, and be joyous little players in the sun.

In a corner Rebecca and Sarah Mary had their play-
house; they were "partners."

"I know somethin'!" sang Sarah Mary, bursting with
the joy of what she knew, "about Christmas. THERE'S
GOIN' TO BE DOLLS! A trustee said it. 'Dolls,' she said,
just like that!"

"Oh!" breathed Rebecca. "But I don't suppose she said one APIECE—"

"She did! She said 'every orphan,' an' that's one apiece! An old lady left some money because once SHE wanted a doll an' didn't anybody know it. An' guess who's goin' to dress 'em."

"Oh, I can't wait to guess!"

Sarah Mary edged closer.

"A—live—dressmaker!"

"A live—WHAT?"

There was actual awe in Rebecca's voice.

"Dressmaker—in pieces o' silk an' satin an' TRIM-MIN'S!"

Rebecca sat very still. She felt that beautiful Christmas doll warm against her little-mother breast. If she rocked gently—like this—and sang a soft hushaby, her baby would go to sleep! In its silky-satin little dress!

Sarah Mary was chattering on. "I was helpin' Ellen carry the lemonade in for the trustees. Somebody said, 'Sh—little pitchers!' That was me. They were afraid I'd hear, an' I did! The dressmaker is a relation to the person-that-wanted-a-doll-once; and she said—the dressmaker—she'd make the dresses for her part. Don't you hope yours will be sky-blue, Rebecca?"

"Oh, yes, sky-blue!" thrilled Rebecca. *Though red would be lovely, or goldy yellow, or green. If she didn't have ANY color dress, I'd love her,* Rebecca thought, rocking her darling-to-be in the tender cradle of her arms.

For ten days Rebecca thought of the Christmas doll by day, and dreamed of it by night. A dozen times she named it. Sweet—Love—Delight—Joy—a dozen beauteous names. The tenth day she settled upon Joy. Her little silk child, Joy!

The eleventh day Rebecca saw the picture. It seemed to start up out of all her happy dreamings and dangle before her eyes—"Look! look at me! Look at my dreadful little orphans!" And Rebecca looked with shocked and horror-stricken eyes. The picture stayed right there, dangling. Nights, too, she could see it. A visitor to the home had brought the paper and read to the children about the hungry orphans across the sea, who were glad for just one meal a day. How contented, then, the visitor had said, ought these orphans at the St. Luke Home to be with their breakfasts and dinners and suppers!

When she went away, she left the paper; and in it Rebecca saw the picture. A score of thin, sad little faces looked out at her. Such hungry faces! One smiled a little, and the smiling hungry face hurt most.

They are orphans, too; I'm kind of a relation to them, thought Rebecca. *But I'm never hungry. Oh, never!* She could not feel herself that kind of "relation." One night she went without her supper, and lay in the dark on her cot in the row of little cots, trying how it felt to be hungry. If she hadn't had that apple between meals—probably those other orphans never had apples between. Perhaps if she didn't eat any breakfast tomorrow. But at breakfast Rebecca ate her bowl of cereal eagerly. She could hardly wait for the breakfast bell. It was terrible to be hungry! That night Rebecca dreamed of her Christmas doll, but it was made of bread. A bread child that she rocked in her arms! And a score of sad little children stood round her as she rocked, and the smiling one broke Rebecca's heart, so that—in the dream—she held her Joy-child out to her, and said, "You may eat her—my beautiful child!"

The picture first, and then the plan. Rebecca made that plan with sweating little soul—it was such a bitter, hard plan to make!

There was so little time left. Anxiously she watched her chance, but it was two days before Christmas before it came. She was sent down town on an errand, and as a special favor given permission to "look in the windows." That meant she need not hurry. She could do her own errands, too.

She was a little scared. It wouldn't be exactly . . . easy. A great automobile stood before a toy shop, and a lady was preparing to alight. She was going in to buy a doll for her little girl! Rebecca read it all instantly, for she was Rebecca.

"Wait! Oh, if you'd only just as LIEVES wait! I—I've got one to sell—I mean a doll for your little girl. With a silk dress that a real live dressmaker made! If you'd just as LIEVES buy mine—"

The small earnest face gazed upward into the surprised face of the lady. There was no doubting the child's seriousness of purpose, however wild her words sounded. The lady was interested.

"May I see it—the dolly you have to sell?" she said smilingly.

A faint pink color surged into Rebecca's cheeks, and deepened to red.

"I haven't got her yet. You—you'll have to trust me to deliver her Christmas. If you'd only as LIEVES trust me!" cried Rebecca.

"My dear! Suppose you come up here into the car, and sit down beside me, and tell me all about it."

"Yes'm—oh, yes'm, I will. It won't start, will it, while I'm getting in? I never was in one before."

On the broad, soft seat Rebecca drew a long breath. Then quite simply she explained the plan.

"So I've got to get some money to buy bread," she concluded wistfully. "Do you think a doll would buy quite a lot? A SILK doll that a dressmaker dressed? If—if you were going to buy your little girl a silk doll, would you think a dollar'd be a great deal to pay?" Oh, a dollar was a great deal! But a great deal of bread was needed. And bread had gone up; the matron said so. Rebecca set her lips firmly.

"I've got to ask a great deal for my chi—I mean, doll. An' I'm going to sell my orange an' stockin' o' candy, too; we always have those at St. Luke's Christmas."

The lady's eyes, gazing backward through the years, were seeing the crumpled pink face of the little girl who had not lived long enough for dolls or Christmas candles. "My dear," the lady said gently, "I will buy your dolly. Here is the dollar. Now shall I drive you to St. Luke's? You are from St. Luke's Orphanage, aren't you?"

"Yes'm, I'm a St. Luke orphan, an' I'd like to be driven, thank you, but I've got two places to stop at first."

"We will stop; tell us where. You may start now, James."

To Rebecca, the "St. Luke orphan," that ride was a

thrilling adventure, so thrilling that she forgot her two stopping places entirely; and the big car had to turn about and retrace its swift, glorious way.

"Are you afraid? Shall I ask James to go slower?"

"Oh, don't! Oh, I mean, please don't ask James!" Rebecca's cheeks were scarlet, her eyes like stars. "I love to fly this way!" Rebecca craned an eager neck, and shouted to the lady above the whir of the car and her whirring little heart, "Do you—s'pose—James—would drive clear—up?"

"Clear up?"

"Yes'm—to St. Luke's door, so they could see me, 'specially Sarah Mary. If James would just as lieves—"

"James would 'just as lieves,' " the lady said with a smile.

The fruitman's was the first stop. Rebecca stepped down carefully, and stated her amazing errand to him with perfect simplicity.

"Will you buy an orange?" she said clearly. "It will be a nice orange, I think. I'll deliver it Christmas morning, but if you'd just as lieves pay for it now—"

Over Rebecca's head the foreigner's eye caught that of the Lady of the Automobile, and some message appeared to travel to him across the short space—over Rebecca's head. It was as if the Lady of the Automobile said to him, "Buy the orange; I will make it all right." She seemed a rich lady, and the automobile was very grand and big—and the risk was very small.

"If it is not too much a price," the man said gravely.

"Oh! Oh, just a—a loaf of bread!" Rebecca stammered nervously. "Could you pay as much as that? I need the bread—I mean THEY need—"

Was the Lady of the Automobile holding up ten fingers? The man went into his little store, and came back. Into Rebecca's hand he dropped two nickels. And Rebecca never knew that the lady dropped two into his.

"He was a nice fruitman," Rebecca said, and added shyly: "an' you were ve-ry nice. I'm glad everybody's nice—I kind of dreaded it. I never expected to have a beautiful time!" She jingled her money joyously. "It must be quite a lot o' bread, it makes so much noise!" she laughed.

At a candy store the lady accompanied Rebecca. Once more a message flashed silently over the child's head. The remarkable advance sale of a Christmas "stockin' o' candy" was accomplished without difficulty.

"Why, so was SHE nice! Now I can take the money to the orphans," Rebecca cried. "I know the way; that visitor told us."

And to the whimsical fancy of the lady it would hardly have been unexpected if Rebecca had gravely asked if James would just as lieves take her overseas to lay this unique gift of bread before the hungry children themselves.

"I'm glad it will buy a lot of bread; they're very hungry orphans. One of them is smiling—I couldn't SMILE could you? But perhaps the orphans over the sea are courageouser. Than St. Luke orphans, I mean. I couldn't hardly WAIT for my breakfast——" Rebecca broke off at that shameful little memory. Oh, these other orphans had to wait!

At the Relief Headquarters Rebecca went in alone. She did not talk much to her new acquaintance the rest of the way back to the St. Luke Orphanage. And she had forgotten her desire to show off to Sarah Mary. It had come suddenly to Rebecca that it was her dear child Joy she had left behind her. A great anguish grew within her—the anguish of affection. Her JOY was dead.

The matron of St. Luke's had always maintained that Rebecca Dill was a very DIFFERENT orphan from the rest. The queer notions that child took! And now this notion to have her Christmas doll—how did she know there was going to be one?—tied up tight in a paper bag—

"If you'd just as lieves," Rebecca pleaded. "I don't

want to see her. I mean it would be EASIER. With a string tied 'round the top."

But Rebecca was not to be present at the Christmas Eve celebration at the St. Luke Orphanage. She was feverish and so nearly sick that the matron decided she must stay in bed. It was Sarah Mary who carried her up the doll (her beautiful, darling child!) in the paper bag, and the candy and the orange. It was to Sarah Mary that Rebecca entrusted the delicate mission of "delivering" them all the next morning to their separate owners.

"Aren't you goin' to LOOK at it, Rebecca Dill? Not PEEK?" It was all very puzzling and unheard of to Sarah Mary. "Mine slept with me last night, right in my bed. I could hear her silk dress creakin' in the dark."

"Mine creaked, too," whispered Rebecca, though of course it might have been the paper bag. "She slept with me, an' I kissed her through a little teeny hole." Rebecca did not say that she had poured her anguished, torn young soul through that "teeny" hole—that she had cried: "Oh, my beloved little child, how can I let you go? Oh, my sweetest, never forget your mother loved you!"

On Christmas afternoon came the Automobile Lady

to St. Luke's. She was a flushed and starry-eyed lady. In her hand she had a curious paper bag, tied at the top. Would the matron send it up to the little Rebecca-orphan, who, it seemed, was sick? Surely not very sick—

"A little feverish, that's all; children often are," the matron said. And the lady smiled gratefully at the reassurance.

"I can go and see her?" she asked. "Not just yet—in a few minutes."

Up in her bed Rebecca tremblingly opened the paper bag. But first she read a "teeny" dangling note.

The dolly I bought for my little girl—will my little girl love it as I am going to love her?
THE AUTOMOBILE LADY

And under the signature Rebecca found a tiny postscript—oh, a beautiful, dear postscript!

If you'd just as lieves be my little girl—

Guest in

the House

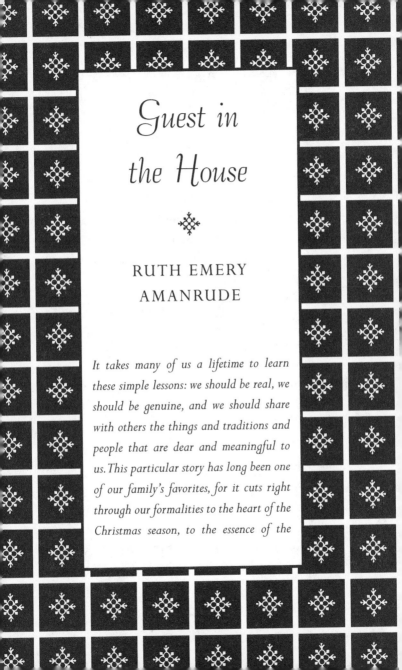

RUTH EMERY
AMANRUDE

*It takes many of us a lifetime to learn
these simple lessons: we should be real, we
should be genuine, and we should share
with others the things and traditions and
people that are dear and meaningful to
us. This particular story has long been one
of our family's favorites, for it cuts right
through our formalities to the heart of the
Christmas season, to the essence of the*

holiday: the celebration once again of the birth, life, death, and
resurrection of our Lord.

Joe's reaction to the pink Christmas tree was a flat and stubborn "No!" And she had been doing it all for him, too, just so they could make a nice impression on the Widdams, but that Joe was such a stick-in-the-mud.

Edie had started to plan the special Christmas Eve the night Joe first told her he wanted Clarice and Ed Widdam for Christmas. Even while she was protesting that the house was too small and too plain to entertain their so-phisticated new neighbors, she was working on her list.

She *had* to make a good impression. The Widdams were obviously people who did things the right way. Their new rambler house was the ramblingest in the neighbor-hood; their attached garage held two shining cars. Just meeting smartly dressed Clarice Widdam in the supermar-ket made Edie feel all helter-skelter and almost dowdy. And Joe wanted the Widdams for Christmas Eve.

"They were tickled, honey," Joe told Edie when she reminded him again that their own Collins family Christmas was so old-fashioned. "This is their first Christmas here since Ed was transferred, and they haven't been here long enough to really know anybody. And Ed loves kids, Edie! He even wants to help out coaching one of the kid baseball teams this summer."

"Oh, goody," Edie said bitingly, "that's how we'll entertain them, then. We'll have a ball game. With Uncle Maynard and Aunt Helen and Cousin Fred, we'll have just enough for a team!" Edie was furious with Joe. Any other time she would have been delighted—but Christmas!

There would be Uncle Maynard and Aunt Helen, each with the latest in aches and pains and their respective remedies. Joe's cousin, Fred, a most uninteresting but kindly soul, would come with his drugstore-wrapped parcels and his wordy explanations of why the large-sized colognes were really the practical buy. The children would be wound up like tops and every good manner and really natural charm would be lost in the mix-up.

Everything for Edie started with a list, so she wrote down every detail of a simple but charmingly served dinner. She planned the children's time so they would not get out of hand. She had revised, rewritten, replanned, and reorganized until the list was perfect. And now she couldn't find it!

"Where did I put it?" she asked herself desperately as

she ransacked all the known tuck-away places in the house. Maybe the children would know. They certainly could find anything else that was hidden away.

"Connie!" Edie really didn't expect an answer, because eleven-year-old Connie had a deafness that could be turned on and off according to the tone of her mother's voice. Today she responded promptly and she trailed in dragging four feet of shower curtain behind her.

"Connie, what in the world are you supposed to be?" Again expecting no answer, Edie went on, "Have you seen my list?"

"Which one?" Connie asked absently as she posed before the wall mirror. "What list are you talking about?"

"The list of things to do for Christmas. I can't find anything in this clutter."

The living room did have that Friday-afternoon look, plus a little extra disorder of the rewrapped gift parcels brought home from school parties. This was the Friday before Christmas, but more important to Edie, it was the Friday before the Widdams!

"I see Bill has been home, too," Edie muttered, glancing at a pair of ice skates, a wad of damp towels, and something that looked like a rusty trap lying just inside the living room door. "To him, home is just one big closet."

"Billy's walking a girl home," giggled Connie, now completely swathed in shower curtain.

"That's nice," Edie drawled. "I hope she inspires him to comb his hair and tuck in his shirttail."

"She's drippy, and so is Bill." Now Connie had one of Edie's brass candlesticks aloft in one hand.

"Okay, Connie, I give up! What are you, the Statue of Liberty?"

"Mother! Don't you know a wise man when you see one?" Connie was shocked with her mother's lack of appreciation.

"Nope, I guess not! I don't get to meet many wise men—not lately, anyway."

"This is a *Bible* wise man! It's for the church play! You forgot!"

Oh, dear, I almost did, Edie thought, but she said, "Not really, dear. Do you know your part?"

"Mine and everyone else's, too," retorted Connie in the know-it-all tone that Edie found unbearable at times. "Is this how a wise man should look, Mom?"

"Exactly, dear, and now please *be* one and remember where you saw the list."

"I saw it in your hand, that's where, and I think it's silly. A list for what we do at Christmas! We always do the same things!" Now she was Connie again, and the shower curtain was just a shower curtain.

That's just the trouble, thought Edie, *we always do the same things.* But this year *had* to be different. She'd *have* to make a new list, that's all.

The sound of the piano in the playroom started. "Oh, no," she groaned, "not that again!"

Two months ago, eight-year-old Carol had balked like a young mule at every reminder to practice her piano lessons. Suddenly, it was different. She had burst into the house two weeks ago, brown eyes shining, crying, "I have a special piece! For two hands! With runs 'n' everything!"

To Edie, Carol's lessons proved no musical ability, merely showed her to be ambidextrous, with her left and right hands working completely independent of each other. Sometimes Edie was sure they were playing two different pieces. But Carol plugged along, counting her one-and-ah, two-and-ah's almost as loudly as she played those un-matched notes. Today it was *too* much.

"Carol! Carol, please!" Edie had to wait for the two-and-ah before she could be heard. Surprisingly, Carol's square little figure appeared promptly.

"Hi, Mom. Where you been? We had a party at school, and we each got a autograph book from Miss Buckley, and we brought home our decorations for our own tree!"

And there they were, wrapped in her sturdy little arms—yards and yards of orange-red paper links! *Oh, no,* thought Edie, *not* orange!

"They're very pretty, honey," Edie said evenly, "but wouldn't you like to have them in the playroom instead?"

"Oh, no, Mom! They're for everyone, not just me! Connie has so many more things on the tree than I do."

Carol's voice told how much the crudely made chain meant to her, and Edie could picture the dark, shining head bent over the task of making this "for everyone."

"Of course, honey. We'll keep it with all the other Christmas things." Edie resolved to find some place for the chain, Widdams or no Widdams.

The big box taken from the storage closet each year held a wealth of these treasures, each marked carefully: BILLY, FIRST GRADE, or CONNIE, KINDERGARTEN, and so on. Each Christmas found the keepsakes a little more worn and defaced but a little more precious.

The box presented a real problem for Edie this year, because the first item on her list had been the pink Christmas tree. That's when Joe shot sparks.

"Whoever heard of a pink Christmas tree!" His nice,

167

Irishy face was anything but nice right then. "Listen, Edie, the Widdams are coming here to spend *our* Christmas in *our* way. That does not include a pink Christmas tree!"

"Oh, Joe, just once can't we do something with a little flair to it?" Edie begged. Joe was unmovable.

"Honey, you can flair all over the place, but you know the kids have had their eyes on a tree in Carlson's woods for a long time. The tree-chopping trip is a part of Christmas, and the kids love it. And so do I. No pink Christmas tree!"

"All right, then. Be stubborn. You know I'm planning everything just for the Widdams." Her voice was at the near-tear stage, and her cheeks were flushed.

"Well, my pet, you can *un*plan everything, then. It's Christmas the old way." And Joe's voice said that ended that.

So it was going to be the regular, ordinary green Christmas tree with Connie's kindergarten angel and Bill's lopsided stars made from tin-can covers and Carol's orange-red chain and all the other off-colored contributions with their dabs of paste and fingerprints still showing.

It isn't that we'd never use them again, Edie's conscience whispered. *It's just that this year was to be so special!*

Joe shot more sparks over the menu. "What do you mean, roast beef?" he asked as he read the list over her shoulder. "What's the matter with *lutfisk?*"

"But, Joe, you never liked *lutfisk* when we were first married," Edie protested. "And the smell!"

"Well, I like it now—smell and all!" Joe's voice softened as he went on. "As far as not liking it, honey, it was just that it was new to me. I never had any Christmas traditions until you showed me. Christmas dinner off a menu, that's what I had. And now *lutfisk* is part of our Christmas."

Edie felt a little ashamed because she remembered too that Joe, who had lived in a succession of rooming houses with his widowed father, had never known the warmth of a family Christmas until their marriage. She had loved his delight and surprise as each new tradition had been introduced, and she had felt a little proud that she could bring a real Christmas feeling into his life.

So, the list had been changed: Green Christmas tree. *Lutfisk*.

A banging in the hall interrupted her thoughts. Bill's half-bass, half-treble voice called out, "We're home!"

"You're telling me," she muttered, but she called, "Welcome! You can start in by putting away your share of the loot stowed around here!"

"You sound crabby, Mom," Bill said as he added a cap and jacket to the mound on the floor.

"I'm in a boy-eating mood, my lad, so do as you're told. You too," she added as she helped five-year-old Rog with his snowsuit.

Oh, dear, she thought as they went up the stairs. *Don't let me get owly over this.*

Friday night was meeting night for everyone but Edie and Rog, so after his bath and story and prayers and three drinks of water, plus a last-minute summons to ask if "Santa Claus had any *real* children of his own," Edie was alone. By the time Joe and the children came home, the new list was ready, and there wasn't a thing on it to get excited about. *It'll be the same old Christmas to us, but the* lutfisk *and the decorations will probably make it the most unusual one the Widdams ever spent,* Edie thought grimly as she tumbled into bed beside the sleeping Joe.

Early Saturday morning, Joe and the children went after the tree. Back in two hours, singing noisily, they tramped through the house like a parade. Then the whole family had a hand in decorating. Though Edie pitched in reluctantly, she soon was giggling with the rest over the yield of the treasure box.

"Pretty crummy-looking stable," Bill muttered, but his face shone at the family's staunch denials.

Just let that Clarice Widdam look down her nose at it! Edie thought. Bill placed the crudely carved lamb and burro in front of the stable he had made from wooden cheese boxes.

"Here's my angel! Where does it go?" squealed Connie.

"Same place as always, hon," Joe told her. "Right on top." And he reached up to place the faded and wilting angel in the uppermost branch.

Next came Bill's stars and Carol's orange-red chain, and then round-eyed Rog cried, "My twinklers!" and Edie helped him to reach up with his paper spirals that bounced like springs and really did twinkle with bits of sequins.

One by one, the treasures were discovered anew. The *tomte gabbe*—and Edie was touched to hear Joe tell Rog that this was *not* Santa Claus but a little elf that Edie's mother, Grandma Hanson, had brought from Sweden. The *jul bok,* raggedy now and brittle, but again Edie had to tell the story of how in Sweden every home has a large straw goat in the yard during the holiday season. A space was cleared on the mantel for the *angla spel,* and after the brass was polished, Connie set the four little candles in place, and Joe touched a match to each wick. The *angla spel* was a favorite with the children, and they loved to watch as the heat of the candle flames started the four chubby angels spinning round and round, each with a wand that touched a little brass chime. "Now it *sounds* like Christmas, too," Carol breathed ecstatically.

Then Joe snapped the switch for the lights. "Oh," breathed the children in unison as the soft blues and reds and golds of the tiny lamps were reflected in the shimmering tinsel. "It's the most beautiful tree ever!" *It is pretty,* Edie thought, *but I did want a pink one with silver ornaments!*

Sunday brought Aunt Helen, complete with cold tablets and liniment and worn out from her bus trip from Duluth. Once Uncle Maynard appeared, though, she fell into a lively swap of symptoms that brought a healthy glow to her eyes. She was not to be outdone; whatever ailment he named, she had one more serious!

At least I don't have to worry about entertaining them, thought Edie. *But the Widdams will get one look at us and one whiff of that lutfisk plus Aunt Helen's liniment, and they'll think we came over on the last boat!*

Cousin Fred, always a favorite with the children, arrived with his pockets bulging and his red face wreathed in smiles and quickly escaped to the playroom, where the racket became almost unbearable. Even Joe, who had stoutly defended Carol's musical ability, finally begged her to stop. "You'd think she could play something besides that tune," he complained cheerfully, as a loud one-and-ah was accompanied by a halting run.

Rog darted in and out on mysterious errands. A rope. A knife. Connie wanted to borrow Edie's coral beads. Bill *needed* a flashlight. And so the day went, and suddenly it was Monday and the day of Christmas Eve. The day of the Widdams.

"This one day should have twenty-four hours all between lunch and dinner," Edie said as she rushed through the house. She scarcely had the last bit of holly tacked in place when the Widdams arrived.

Ed Widdam was hearty and friendly, and the children took him over at once. Clarice Widdam smiled sweetly and thanked Edie for allowing them to come. "I told Ed it was almost too much to expect," she said in her soft voice, "but I think the idea of having children around at Christmas was a temptation that overcame his good manners."

"Oh, but we *wanted* you," Edie replied eagerly, and she found herself meaning it.

Clarice was generous in her compliments about the house and the children, and she won Aunt Helen completely with her sympathy. *She's a lady, all right,* Edie thought.

Everything went well, and Joe beamed with pride as the children pointed out the treasures on the tree. "The twinklers are mine," Rog told them proudly, "but they're for everyone."

"And I made the chain," Carol added, "and Connie made the angel when she was only six years old."

"Such a Christmasy angel, too," Clarice Widdam said.

"I'll have to make a new manger next year," Bill said in his half-man voice, and making an awkward attempt to explain the crude stable.

"But you must always keep this one, Bill," Clarice told him. "It's the very first one you made; that makes it special." Edie thanked her silently with her eyes.

The room looked like Christmas. The little *angla spel* tinkled away merrily and the festive glow of the tree shone on the happy faces in the room.

Suddenly Clarice Widdam exclaimed, "What *is* that I smell?"

Edie's heart went plop! *I knew it,* she thought. *Here goes our nice impression!*

"It's *lutfisk,*" Joe said. And he made it sound like pheasant under glass. "We have it every year. It's Scandinavian, you know."

"Indeed I do know," answered Clarice, "and it's years since I've had it." At Edie's look of surprise, Clarice continued, "I'm one of those Minnesota Swedes you hear about, and I used to see the *lutfisk* stacked like cord wood outside my father's grocery store. The weather would be cold enough to keep it until it was taken home and soaked for hours. Then it was trimmed and tied in a cheesecloth bag and cooked in a huge kettle and soon we'd smell it all over the house. That wonderful, wonderful smell!"

Edie felt weak. *And I was for beef,* she thought. "I'm so glad you like it. For us, it wouldn't be Christmas without *lutfisk*—even my big Irishman loves it." And from her big Irishman she received a wry and slightly accusing grin that made her squirm.

"And who wouldn't like it?" asked Clarice, daring anyone to speak up.

Aunt Helen, rejuvenated by the thought of food, added, "And it's so healthy. So easy to digest." Uncle Maynard just nodded and Cousin Fred beamed and said the way he liked *lutfisk* was in large quantities.

And so dinner was a wonderful success. The chatter was gay and familyish, and the Widdams obviously enjoyed everything and everybody. As they left the table, Clarice Widdam said, "This is a Christmas I shall never forget. It is almost as though it were planned just for me."

It was, thought Edie, avoiding Joe's look—*for you, in spite of me and my big ideas.*

"It's time for the program!" sang out Rog as the family and guests settled themselves in the living room.

Every Christmas Eve, right after dinner and before any gifts were opened, the family sang carols and the children performed their parts from the church and school programs. Edie had hoped to postpone this little ceremony until after the guests' departure, and now she murmured, almost apologetically, "They love this part of Christmas."

"Why, of course they do," Clarice's eyes were sparkling and she applauded softly, encouraging the children to begin.

After a few minutes of whispered conference in the hall, Bill entered with a wooden box that he placed carefully at one end of the room. His back was turned, but when he moved aside, they could see the shaded glow of light that came from inside the box.

"It's a cradle," whispered Clarice. "They've made a cradle for their program."

So that's why they wanted a flashlight, Edie thought.

Bill left quietly, and serious little Rog entered. In childish, measured tones he recited his Sunday-school "Welcome One and All" poem and bowed formally during the applause that followed. Still unsmiling, Rog announced, "In a minute, we'll have a play—soon's I put my costume on. I have *two* parts, because there aren't enough of us to *be* everything." He did smile then, but a sibilant whisper from the hall restored his dignity and he went on. "The people in the play are Miss Constance Collins; she's the wise man. Mr. William Collins is the shepherd, and I am—and Mr. Roger Collins is—the angel." At that moment he looked like one. "Miss Carol Collins is the accompa—she plays the piano." He started to leave, but hesitated long enough to say, "We all wrote the play, only Connie did the most."

There was a little flurry of excitement in the hall, and then Carol entered and seated herself with dignity at the piano. She played a halting arrangement of "Silent Night" as the others came in. Connie, resplendent in the shower curtain and with Edie's coral beads holding a silk scarf on her head, led the procession. Thought Edie, *It really doesn't look like a shower curtain now.* In her hands Connie held a long white scroll, and on her face was a look of reverence.

Next came Bill in Joe's striped bathrobe tied with a stout rope around his slim waist. His head was hooded and he carried Carol's old toy lamb under his arm. Rog came last, swathed in white, with two huge paper wings pinned to his back. On his head was a band of tinsel. As he took his place behind the cradle, the glow from within gave an added radiance to his sweet face and made the tinsel band truly a halo.

Connie read the Christmas story from her scroll. The

177

children stood quietly, moving only as the lovely story progressed. They looked at the sky and at the Star everyone felt was really there. They expressed the awe of the shepherds and the wise men. They knelt in adoration before the Manger of the Babe.

And then the piano started again. Edie sat straight and stiff as she recognized the long-practiced melody and she groped for Joe's hand. Carol's fingers seemed so sure, and though her lips counted the one-and-ah, two-and-ah's, she did not miss a note.

Forgive me, Edie thought. *They knew all the time what was really important about Christmas and I almost forgot. To think they had to show me again! It isn't pink Christmas trees or something you can put on a list. It isn't glitter and impressions. It's all this—love and sweetness and sharing.* She felt the understanding pressure of Joe's hand on hers, and with her eyes filled with happy tears, she listened to the children sing.

Sweetly and simply, their voices rang out in the words. "Happy Birthday to You. Happy Birthday to You. Happy Birthday, Dear Jesus, Happy Birthday to You."

Roses in December

�֍

SYBIL HADDOCK

Jabez was self-sufficient: he needed no one and didn't wish to be needed by anyone. He was crusty and seemingly devoid of sentiment and warmth.

Then somebody began sending out gifts under his signature—and his doorbell started ringing.

This very old Canadian story had almost vanished from memory; in fact, I have seen only one copy of it in my entire lifetime.

Jabez Oldbury was stepping across the hall of his comfortable home on his way to the conservatory. He paused and listened. From the kitchen came the sound of a voice singing:

> From the eastern mountains,
> Pressing on they come,
> Wise men in their wisdom,
> To His humble home.

Jabez had no ear for music, but that fact did not account for the deep frown he wore between his eyebrows.

He disliked Christmas, and he hated to be reminded of the festive season. The words of the Christmas hymn made him feel as one supposes a cat feels when its fur stands on end at the sight of a dog.

There was something about Christmas that always made Jabez feel like that, and he never failed to remark that he was thankful when it was over.

People did such idiotic things that they would never dream of doing at any other time. They gave without discrimination; they helped people without first finding out whether they deserved help; folk were foolish and sentimental at Christmas. Jabez was never sentimental, and he never gave anything away unless he was sure of getting its equivalent back again—or more. To his wealthy friends who were in need of nothing he gave expensive gifts. If he knew he would only get a card, he sent a card. It had never occurred to him to distribute his gifts in any other way, and somehow he never got out of Christmas what other people seemed to get.

It simply made him feel more irritable than usual, and he wished his housekeeper would not sing about it. At the same time it was impossible for him to ask her not to sing about Christmas, for Mrs. Simpson was worth her weight in gold to Jabez, and he knew it.

His house was perfectly kept, and as far as it was possible with a man like Jabez for its master, Mrs. Simpson had made it a home as well as a house.

The frown Jabez was wearing grew deeper as he realized that he must put up with the singing, much as he disliked it. He turned to continue his journey to the conservatory, when through the opaque glass in the front door he saw something. It was somebody lifting a hand to ring the bell. Jabez strode to the door and flung it open.

On the step stood a woman whom he had often seen in the village a mile from his house. Her shabby clothes were not of recent fashion, and she breathed heavily, as though she had been running.

Jabez wondered snobbishly what she was doing at his front door, surely the tradesman's entrance was the place for her. That thought flashed through his mind, and then vanished. It was banished by something more amazing.

Jabez forgot everything except the expression in the eyes of the woman who was looking at him. Never in his fifty years had any person looked at him in the same way. Jabez could not define the strange feeling it gave him, but in a subconscious way he knew that he liked it. For a moment they stared at one another. Jabez amazed, the woman breathless. Then, "Oh, sir," she gasped, "I couldn't rest till I'd thanked you."

"Thanked me!" exclaimed Jabez, "what——"

"The money'll set my boy up, sir, and—and——"

"My good woman," Jabez began, and then, to his great discomfort, his amazing visitor burst into tears. Whilst her face worked with emotion she could not control, she seized his hand, shook it as it had never been shaken before, pushed her hat more firmly onto her head, and rushed away. Jabez stood there, by his own front door, looking utterly foolish, too astonished to do anything but open and close his mouth like a fish out of water.

He had not the faintest idea what the woman had been talking about.

He smoothed the place on his head where he should have had hair, straightened his tie, patted his coat, and turned toward the kitchen from whence came that irritating singing. He opened the kitchen door.

"Mrs. Simpson," he said, "do you know a Mrs. Trim who lives in the village!"

Mrs. Simpson looked up from a sheet she was mending. It dawned on Jabez for the first time that she hardly looked like a housekeeper. One associated such a lady with black clothes and a prim and proper air. Mrs. Simpson wore neither. Her gray skirt and pullover were becoming to her snow-white hair that curled in a delightful fashion around her face. It was a pity she had to wear horn-rimmed glasses; they disfigured her.

"Yes, I do," she said.

"Did you know she was at the door?"

"No, I didn't hear anybody. I was singing, and Amelia's out."

"You're too kind to that girl. You let her go out too often."

"She does her work well, and we're only young once, you know," replied Mrs. Simpson, smiling.

"Yes, I suppose we are," agreed Jabez. "It was that Mrs. Trim at the door," he went on. "She comes to clean for Miss Merton, doesn't she?"

Mrs. Simpson carefully fixed a patch.

"Yes," she said, "twice a week."

"Is she crazy?" asked Jabez, standing, tall and thin as a barber's pole, by the lintel of the door.

"I should say she certainly isn't. Though she's had enough trouble to drive her crazy."

"Has she?" said Jabez indifferently. "Then, I think, in spite of what you say, it must have affected her brain. She's been here and talked no end of rubbish. I couldn't make head or tail of it. Do you mind sending her away if she comes again."

"Very well," said Mrs. Simpson.

Jabez went back into the hall and down the short passage leading to his conservatory. As soon as he stepped into it he heaved a great sigh of contentment, and forgot all about Mrs. Trim and everybody else. For the roses that Jabez had in December were his joy and pride. They were no more lovely than roses that grow in June, but the fact that he—assisted by his gardener—grew them in December, when nobody else had any, gave Jabez peculiar satisfaction.

He had taken off his coat and rolled up his shirt-

186

sleeves ready to spray some of the blooms, when a door leading from the garden opened, and a small old lady limped in, tapping her way with a stick. She wore a black dress of ancient cut, but expensive material, an ugly, flat black hat, and an air of determination.

"Hullo!" said Jabez, going on with his work.

" 'Hullo!' your grandmother," retorted his visitor. "Are you mad, Jabez?"

"Mad?" queried Jabez, pausing with one hand on a flowerpot. "Why?"

Miss Merton lived next door to Jabez, and was an old lady of decided views that she never hesitated to state. "Don't be an idiot, Jabez," she said, "I mean Mrs. Trim."

Jabez put down the syringe he had been intending to use, and looked down at his neighbor like an eagle regarding a very impertinent sparrow.

"I haven't the faintest idea," he said, "what you're talking about. All I do know is that Mrs. Trim is crazy."

"If being crazy makes Mrs. Trim see ten pound notes," replied Miss Merton, "then I dare say there are other people who would like to be crazy."

"If Mrs. Trim has seen ten pound notes, I don't know what that has to do with me."

"Only that you gave them to her."

"I—gave—I—what?" stammered Jabez.

187

"Mrs. Trim received a registered envelope addressed in your writing, containing your name inside, and ten pound notes, this morning. She rushed—"

Amelia opened the door.

"You're wanted on the phone, please, sir," she said.

"I can't come," snapped Jabez. "Take the message."

"The lady insists on speaking to you, sir."

"Go along, Jabez," suggested Miss Merton. "I'll come, and finish telling you after—hurry up!"

"Forgetting his coat, Jabez hurried into the hall, leaving Miss Merton to follow more slowly.

"Jabez Oldbury speaking," he barked into the receiver.

"Oh, Mr. Oldbury," came a feminine voice, "I really don't know how to thank you. You don't know what such a gift means at this time of the year."

"You've got the wrong number," said Jabez.

"You're Mr. Jabez Oldbury?"

"Yes—yes—but—"

"So sorry, there's a bad case just come in. I'm wanted. Many, many thanks."

Furiously, Jabez rang up the exchange, and found that it was the matron of a hospital who had been speaking to him.

"Now what's the matter?" demanded Miss Merton.

"I think," replied Jabez, "that there must be some escaped lunatics about today. That was somebody thanking
me for something I don't know anything about—I don't
even know what she was thanking me for, and whatever it
was, I didn't do it."

"Of course you didn't," agreed Miss Merton.

"How do you know I didn't?" roared Jabez angrily.

"You've just said you didn't, you old idiot," replied his
neighbor calmly. "Besides, you wouldn't. You're not that
sort."

"Well, now," said Jabez, "perhaps you'll be kind
enough to finish telling me—"

"Excuse me, sir," remarked Amelia, appearing at that
moment. "Sam Jackson's at the back door. He wants to
speak to you."

"Sam Jackson? Who is Sam Jackson?" demanded
Jabez, who by this time was getting really irritable.

"He keeps that little shop at the bottom of the lane,
sir," replied Amelia.

"I'll wait," said little Miss Merton, and tapping
her way into the dining room with her stick, she sat by the
fire.

Jabez strode angrily to the back door. He was opening his mouth to growl at the man who stood there, when
he noticed exactly the same expression in his eyes that had

been in Mrs. Trim's, and Jabez could not say anything. He was acutely conscious of nothing but that wonderful look. He basked in it like a sun-starved child basking in the sun. In a half conscious fashion he heard the man thanking him for paying a doctor's bill of which he had never heard, but all Jabez wanted was that the man should go on looking at him for a long time. Jabez stammered something. Sam Jackson gripped his hand and walked away. In a half-dazed fashion Jabez made his way back to the dining room and sank into the nearest chair.

"Well?" said Miss Merton.

"He wanted to thank me for paying a doctor's bill that I've never heard of," said Jabez.

"What did you say?"

"I . . . nothing . . . I . . ."

The front door bell rang. Without waiting for Amelia, and still without his coat, Jabez hurried to the door. Somebody had put a letter through the letter slot and it was on the floor. Jabez picked it up, and slit it open.

The Thatches.
Dec. 20th.

Dear Mr. Oldbury,

Many thanks for the lovely roses. God does indeed give us memory that we may have roses in

December. I hope the December of your life may be filled with roses.

Yours very gratefully,
Sarah Spencer

It was too much. His own gardener must have been giving away some of his beloved roses! Forgetting all about Miss Merton, Jabez dashed once more down the passage leading to the conservatory, and collided violently with a little man coming in the opposite direction. It was Ben, the gardener.

"Oh!" he gasped, clutching his nose, which was prominent, and had been nearly flattened.

"What do you mean by it?" roared Jabez.

"I couldn't 'elp it, sir. You was runnin' an' I was runnin' an—"

"What do you mean by giving away my roses, I mean?"

If Ben had been accused of giving away the clothes of his own body, he could not have looked more astounded. "Why, sir," he gasped, "I'd sooner think o' flyin'." There was no doubt of Ben's innocence. He carried it on his face.

"And I was comin' to thank you, sir," he added.

"Thank me!" exclaimed Jabez. "Good gracious, man, what for?"

"For the money for my new teeth."

"Money? Teeth? Come into the dining room and show me."

Ben followed his master, and from somewhere about his person he produced an envelope, addressed apparently by Jabez Oldbury, the envelope contained five pound notes, and the curt command written, again apparently by Ben's master, GET SOME NEW TEETH.

"These is always fallin' out, sir," remarked Ben, "an' I'm very much obliged to you. Teeth is awful expensive."

Before Jabez could recover from his astonishment, Ben had gone, and Miss Merton was showing her own excellent teeth in a wide smile.

"Read that," commanded Jabez, pushing the letter that he had found in the hall across the table.

Miss Merton read the note slowly.

"Christmas roses," she murmured thoughtfully. "Jabez, there's somebody anxious to make out that you're everything you're not."

"What do you mean?" sputtered Jabez.

"Somebody is trying to make other people believe that you're kind and generous and Christmassy and all that sort of thing."

"And am I not?"

"Don't be a fool," snapped his neighbor. "You know you're not."

"Then why should anybody want to make out that I am?" asked Jabez, rubbing his bald head in a bewildered fashion.

"Goodness knows," replied Miss Merton. "That's what puzzles me. It's a waste of time and money, because you'll just go round to these people tomorrow and say you didn't do it, and that's that."

"What?" Jabez snapped out the word and closed his mouth like a rat trap.

He was thinking how hateful it would be to see that light go out of Mrs. Trim's eyes, out of Sam's eyes, and Ben's eyes.

"It's the only thing you can do," continued Miss Merton.

"Well . . . er . . . yes," stammered Jabez.

"You look like a worried walnut," remarked Miss Merton, "with your face all wrinkled up like that. Go and get your coat on."

"Sally," said Jabez, "did you do it?"

"Did I do what?"

"Did you give this money away in my name?"

"The person who did," replied Miss Merton, "is either

a saint or a fool. I'm not sure which, and I'm neither. No, Jabez, I didn't. Put your coat on and walk across the garden with me."

The next morning there were six letters by the first post thanking Jabez for gifts of money about which he knew nothing. "Amelia," he said, "where does Mrs. Trim live?"

"Rose Cottage, sir."

Amelia was packing the breakfast things on a tray.

"What's been her trouble?" asked Jabez.

"Her husband was ill and out of work for months, then he died; and then Jim, her only boy, who was earning a few shillings a week, he got knocked down by a car and nearly killed. It never rains but it pours, sir."

"Seems like it," agreed Jabez. "My shoes clean?"

Jabez knocked at the door of Rose Cottage quite determined to tell Mrs. Trim the truth. As that lady opened the door, he opened his mouth, but the words he meant to say would not come. At sight of him that wonderful light leaped into Mrs. Trim's eyes, and Jabez could not put it out. Before he knew where he was he found himself in a spotless kitchen where a boy about sixteen sat by the fire.

"Here's Mr. Oldbury, Jim," said Mrs. Trim.

Jim blushed and stammered.

Jabez blushed and stammered.

194

Mrs. Trim came to the rescue by remarking, "He'll be able to go away now, sir, your money'll cure him."

"You'll go, too, of course?" said Jabez, recovering a little.

"Me? No, sir. The money'll keep one person away longer than two."

Jabez drew what Mrs. Trim afterward called "a queer book" from his pocket, wrote in it, tore out a paper, handed it to her, growled, "Take that to the bank. They'll give you some money. You go away, too."

Before the astonished woman, or her son, could recover, Jabez had fallen over the cat; kicked over the milk jug that stood on the step; and was flying down the lane as though pursued by demons, but feeling a strange happiness he had never known before.

He went to Sam Jackson's shop, and when he left he knocked over a bottle of pickled onions that stood on the counter, and kicked a box of eggs from one end of the shop to the other, but he left behind a check and two very grateful hearts, one belonging to Sam, the other to his wife. When Jabez got home, Miss Merton was waiting for him.

"Well?" she said.

"Well?" replied Jabez.

"You told them?"

"No, I didn't."

"What?" Miss Merton peered over the top of her glasses.

"I didn't, I said."

"Then what did you say?" demanded Miss Merton. "You know Mrs. Trim chars for me. She'll tell me, if you don't."

"Let her tell you, then," replied Jabez. "I'm going to see Mrs. Spencer."

Mrs. Spencer was an invalid, but she was not poor. In her room Jabez found a bunch of exquisite roses, and beside them a Christmas card, with another bunch of roses, and the words GOD GIVES US MEMORY, THAT WE MAY HAVE ROSES IN DECEMBER.

"I liked the card," said Mrs. Spencer, "as much as the flowers."

"The words are beautiful," agreed Jabez, not really thinking of them, but wondering where those lovely blooms could have come from, and while he was wondering, Mrs. Spencer was talking—

"It's a beautiful idea," she was saying, "and there are other roses for December besides sweet memories, and memories of kind deeds, aren't there?"

"Are there?" Jabez was still thinking of the real roses.

"Well, my children are my December roses," replied

the invalid. "What should I do now—in the December of my life without them?"

Jabez started like a man walking from a dream. Once he had been in love, but not even for love had Jabez been prepared to take any risks. He hadn't, he thought at that time, enough money to marry. So little Ann, with her dark, curling hair, her gray eyes that were like sea seen through mist, had faded out of his life.

"I—never thought of children like that," he stammered. "I always thought of them as—well—a responsibility—a burden."

"Their backs are strong when ours are weak. I shouldn't have mentioned it if you hadn't sent me these roses. I'm sorry if I've touched a tender spot."

"You've only made me realize what a fool I've been," growled Jabez. Then, as he stumbled in his usual clumsy way out of the house, he added, "I'll send some more roses."

Miss Merton was watching from her window for Jabez, and as he passed she beckoned to him to come in. "Well," she said, "did you find out anything?"

"Yes," snapped Jabez.

"What?" barked the little old lady, sitting up suddenly like a Jack-in-the-box.

"That I'm a fool."

"My dear man, I mean something I didn't know. Why, I've been telling you that for years. Did you find out who the Christmas rose person is?"

"No, I didn't."

Miss Merton peered at Jabez over her glasses. "Do you know," she said, "what I should think if it weren't too absurd? I should think if I didn't know it was impossible, that there's somebody who loves you."

"Don't be a . . . don't be funny," growled Jabez.

"Don't mind what you call me," said Miss Merton, knitting busily. "If you're rude to me, I can always be rude to you."

Jabez grinned broadly. "I know you can," he said.

"My dear old idiot," went on the old lady, "some wise person has managed to make you realize that you're missing a lot in life—you've always snapped my head off if I tried to tell you. I suppose I've gone the wrong way about it; you'll find when December comes that you'll wish you'd grown more Christmas roses, I know."

Jabez stood over the fireplace.

"I know. I've seen Mrs. Trim."

"I've started to grow them," he growled.

Suddenly Miss Merton leaned across and put a withered hand on Jabez's knee. "Take my advice," she said, "don't rest till you find out who's done it."

Then she stood up and patted the bald spot on his head. "Good night, Jabez," she said.

"Good night, Sally," he replied, getting up to open the door for her.

The earth was covered with white frost and a big round moon rode in a cloudless sky as Jabez made his way over his neighbor's garden into his own. It was very late when he went to bed that night, and it was not until he was undressing that he missed a small notebook from his pocket. It must have slipped out when he took his coat off in the greenhouse, things often did.

He put on his dressing gown and crept down to get it. The conservatory was flooded with moonlight, and Jabez easily found the book, then he stood still breathing the perfume of the roses, looking at the garden asleep under its white blanket of frost. Sound itself was sleeping, and Jabez almost held his breath.

Suddenly his tall figure straightened. Out of the shadows that surrounded his own house a figure appeared; a small figure covered in something dark, and silent as the night. One hand clutched the cloak so that it should not open, and the same hand held a bunch of—Jabez stared—

they looked like—they were—roses. As Jabez opened the greenhouse door the latch clicked; the little figure turned sharply, gasped, and stood still. So did Jabez.

They stood in perfect silence with the moonlight all about them, gazing at one another. Then Jabez stooped, blinked, like somebody who cannot believe what he sees, and looked more closely. Two gray eyes like the sea seen through mist never flinched as he stared into them.

"Ann," he just breathed the little name. "Ann—it can't be—Ann—Mrs. Simpson."

"My hair has gone white, you see, Jabez, and I wore glasses so that you shouldn't know me. Twenty years is a long time. I was always good at housekeeping, so I chose to earn—to work that way."

"You're a widow then?"

Ann shook her head. "I'm Ann Anderson, as I always was."

"Mrs. Simpson?"

"It was easy to get a friend to do all that, Jabez, to give me a reference and put that name in it. Somebody who knew us both in the old days told me you were living here, and you needed a housekeeper, and—and—all about you."

"And these?" Jabez touched the roses.

Ann hesitated for the first time. "These," she said, "are

from—I've hidden them. Amelia's never seen them. And I imitated your writing well, didn't I?"

"Where have they come from?" insisted Jabez.

"They're from my own hothouses."

Jabez gasped. "Your own hothouse? And you've been working as my housekeeper."

Ann nodded, and at the door of Jabez's memory there hammered the words Miss Merton had said that very day— "there must be somebody who loves you."

Jabez reached out two long arms, and put his hands on Ann's shoulders. He turned so that the moonlight fell full upon her face, and the black cloak slipped from her lovely, ruffled hair.

"Why?" he demanded mercilessly. "Why, Ann?"

Her gray eyes never flinched from his.

"You've got everything in life that matters second, Jabez; I wanted you to have everything that matters first. I wanted you to see gratitude in people's eyes; to hear it in their voices. I wanted you to have some roses for December—you've missed some, you know."

"It's worse than that, Ann," he said. "I've made you miss some."

"Yes," she admitted, "you have."

"Ann," said Jabez, "I've been a fool. The biggest fool

ever created. If I waited a long time could you ever bring yourself to forgive me, and to help me to grow a few December roses?"

Ann was not looking at him now; her eyes were fixed on the roses in her hand, and she was very quiet.

"Never mind, dear," said Jabez. "I oughtn't to have said it. It was like my cheek."

Then the two gray eyes, full of laughter and tears, were lifted: "I was thinking," said Ann, "that as you're fifty and I'm forty, it's a pity to wait."

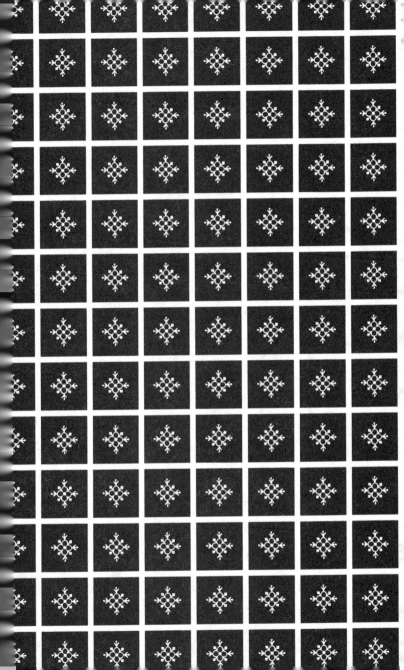

The
Red Mittens

✤

HARTLEY F. DAILEY

Oh, how often we judge a person by the mask, just as we do a house by its façade—and fail to see the treasure inside! There is no better master key than kindness.

Hartley F. Dailey, from Centerville, Ohio, is still writing memorable stories; he has been doing so for nigh unto half a century. One of the serendipities of compiling story anthologies has to do with the *number of living authors who have come into my life as a result; Mr. Dailey has become a cherished friend. Many years ago, he wrote for such magazines as* Sunshine—*now no longer with us. "The Red Mittens" first appeared in it.*

Asked about the origins of this story, Dailey wrote, "As to the 'Red Mittens' story, I spent the years of my early adulthood in the Great Depression. If I write about that, you can be sure I know what I am writing about. The character of Old Man Riggs was taken almost entirely from a man I knew a number of years before the story was written. He was reputed to be a millionaire, but the first time you met him you would have thought he was a pauper. The character of Jane was taken from my wife, and Linda from my daughter Nancy."

I think I really count my Christmases from the year Linda was eight. That is the year when "Peace on earth, good will to men" first began to mean something to me.

That was in '34, the worst year of the Great Depression, at least for farmers. Like many another, I had bought a quarter section, 160 acres, just before the market crash, and at much too high a price. Now, with farm prices at rock bottom, the prices of things we had to buy were rising. It took every cent we could scrape together just to pay the interest on the place.

That was the year we decided we just couldn't afford to buy Christmas presents. For ourselves—Jane and I—we didn't mind, but for Linda, we felt differently. Our only child, she seemed almost a baby. She was a serious-minded little girl, with a wealth of silky brown hair and a pair of enormous brown eyes, so warm they would have melted the heart of the legendary Snow Queen. We felt she was just too young to understand why there was no money to buy presents.

There was a beautiful light-blue coat, just Linda's size, in the window of Lloyd's department store, in the county seat. Every time we'd go to town she'd go and stare into that store window to see if it was still there. But the price was an impossible $12.95! It might just as well have been $100. Jane went to great pains remaking a coat of her own, to fit Linda, and she wore it dutifully. But it could not take the place of the one in Lloyd's window.

In those days our nearest neighbor was Old Man Riggs, whose 500 acres lay between our place and the river. Old Charley Riggs was the stingiest man in three counties, with a disposition like a sour apple and an expression on his face that hinted his chief diet was unripe persimmons. He was reputed to have money, but you never would have guessed it. He dressed like a tramp, and he drove a broken-down old Model T. He never put side-curtains on it, no matter how cold the weather. He'd sit bolt upright, his big, knobby hands holding the steering wheel in a grip like death. I never saw him wear a pair of gloves—not until after that Christmas.

One of the most pressing problems for a farmer in the hill country is water. If you don't have access to a spring or a stream, you must have deep wells to get it. And at that time, before electricity came to the hills, you pumped it by hand. And pumping all the water for all the animals on a farm is labor, indeed.

I had been trying for years to negotiate a right-of-way across Old Man Riggs's place, to the river. Here I was, spending half my time pumping water, while across the narrowest point in Riggs's place, fifty yards from my pasture, was a whole river full! And it wasn't as if he needed it. He had over a mile of frontage—and he wouldn't sell me an inch!

As Christmas approached, Jane was busy going through the attic, picking out things to make, or remake, and for materials to decorate with. Linda was an interested spectator.

Then, one day, she came to me with a suggestion. "I want to give Mr. Riggs a Christmas present!" she said.

I was thunderstruck! But I said, "What could you give Mr. Riggs, Linda?"

"I'd have Mother make him some mittens, like she makes for you," came Linda's confident answer.

"Why," I blurted, "the old man would be too stingy to wear them, if you did."

I saw at once that I had made a mistake, for Linda hung her pretty head, and began making circles with her toe, in a way she had. "Mr. Riggs is my friend," she said. "He lets me eat pears from that big tree in his yard."

I wouldn't have been more surprised if she had said she had trained one of the local wild cats to catch mice in the kitchen. But, knowing her as I did, I shouldn't have been surprised, even at that. Myself, I wouldn't have given the old tightwad the time of day from his own watch, but I couldn't deny Linda anything, when she looked like that. Besides, I saw the hand of Jane in this, for Jane, the gentlest and sweetest of women, has an iron will that brooks no opposition in such matters. I went down on my knees beside Linda and took her in my arms. "Aw, honey," I told her, "if you want to give Mr. Riggs some mittens, you go right ahead!"

Every winter Jane made several pairs of zero-mittens

for me. These were mittens cut from the best parts of my worn-out overalls, and lined with pieces of worn blankets. Then she would knit some cuffs of yarn, and sew them on.

These were the mittens Linda wanted to give to the old neighbor. Jane cut out two pairs for Old Man Riggs, but she left the sewing to Linda. She cut one pair from overalls, but she found an old skirt in the attic—I think the brightest red I ever saw—and she cut one pair from this. When they were finished, they went into a box, along with some of Jane's molasses cookies. Early on Christmas Eve, before dark, Linda took the box and left it on Riggs's porch.

About eleven o'clock next morning, my chores done, I was sitting in the living room while Jane and Linda prepared our Christmas dinner. Suddenly, with a clatter like an earthquake in a tin shop, Old Man Riggs's Model T turned into our drive. He had his usual death grip on the wheel, but on his hands were the flaming red mittens!

He came to an abrupt halt just in front of the house and climbed painfully to the ground. He further mystified me by lifting a big cardboard grocery box from the rear seat. Then he marched right up to the front door, and knocked, holding the box under his arm. After the briefest of greetings, he asked for Linda. When she came in from the kitchen, he put his hand into the box and lifted something out. There, beautiful to behold, was the beloved, fabulous blue coat!

Linda let out a cry of wild delight, and then, after the manner of womankind, she began to sob. Mr. Riggs put his hand caressingly on her head with remarkable gentleness. "You know," he said, "I had a little girl just like you, once, a long time ago. Only her hair was red." He tried to say more, but only his lips moved.

A moment later, Jane came in from the kitchen. And piling surprise upon surprise, Old Man Riggs again reached into his box. What he handed Jane was a hand-tooled leather bag that must have cost fully as much as the coat! Riggs turned to me. "I hope," he growled, "you won't mind if I give your wife a Christmas present, John."

It wasn't just a common courtesy that made me ask Riggs to stay for dinner. The old man began to stammer and make excuses. But Jane would have none of this. "Nonsense," she chided, "we've got plenty for everyone, and it'll be ready in just a little while. Anyway"—she clinched her argument—"I've already set a place for you."

Poor though we were, we never went hungry. The farm yielded an abundance of food, and it was nourishing and good. And Jane was a cook who could make a feast out of the plainest fare. There wasn't a turkey, but there was a fat chicken from our flock, as well as a pair of rabbits I had shot the day before, served, of course, with plenty of Jane's good cornbread dressing. We didn't have tea or coffee, but there were cider and milk aplenty.

I could tell the old man enjoyed the meal. There was a kind of dreamy look in his eyes. Once he looked at Jane, sort of stammered, and then remarked, "A man sorter forgets about a woman's way with food, when he lives by himself."

After the meal, Riggs sat in the living room with me for a while, smoking a pipeful of my home-grown tobacco. But finally he put on his coat and started toward the door. "Gotta be about my chores," he explained. Then suddenly he turned to me and said, "You know, John, there's a place down at the end of my field, where an old road used to go through. If you'll fence that off, and run your stock down over it—it won't cost you a dime."

As he slipped through the door, he waved his red mittens and said, "Merry Christmas, Linda! If you will bring your basket to my house, I'll fill it up with some of them pears for your folks."

Lonely Tree

�֎

MARGARET E. SANGSTER, JR.

Loneliness . . . it's all around us, invading every crevice of our sad land—far more so than was true when this story was written early in this century.

There was a lonely, joyless executive, a lonely growing-old-before-her-time stenographer, and a lonely little crippled boy—and then came Christmas.

Margaret E. Sangster, Jr. (1899–1981) and her illustrious grandmother by the same name wrote some of the most memorable stories of their time. Then, for about half a century, the name Margaret E. Sang-ster was almost forgotten. What a joy to help bring her and her wonderful stories back. "Lonely Tree" is one of her most moving.

There was a pleasant bustle about the long office, a sense of subdued hilarity, of intense eagerness, of dreams coming true. Pretty girls covered their typewriters with ungainly black oilcloth coats; other pretty girls covered their noses with white powder jackets. And all about them surged the little waves of their excited exclamations.

"I'm going home—home," said one girl, "on the two o'clock from Grand Central. It'll be snowing when I get off the train at six—I know it'll be snowing. And Pa'll meet me with the cutter . . ." Her voice was lost in the hum of general conversation.

The tall, thin woman who was head stenographer was talking. There was even a gentle note in her stark voice. "It was kind of nice," she said slowly, "of him"—her head jerked in the direction of the office with the gilt lettering on its plateglass door—"it was kind of nice of him to give us this half-day. It's our busy season now, and he might of—"

The little blonde interrupted. "Fat chance he'd 'a 'ad to make me work this afternoon!" she scoffed. "Fat chance! I got all my shopping ter do. I haven't bought so much as a button! Say, ain't it twelve yet?"

The Lonely Girl, one of the crowd but scarcely a part of it, raised tired eyes from her notebook. So the little blonde hadn't done her shopping yet. And one of the others was going home. And the rest . . . She closed the notebook suddenly; the dots and dashes had begun to blur. It seemed strange that there could be people who had no reason to buy presents, no home to go to. It seemed strange . . .

The plateglass door with its gilt lettering was swinging open, and the hum of conversation died suddenly away. Not that the man who stood in the doorway was a stern man or an unfair one—not that he frightened his employees into a respectful silence. Only—there was something so curiously aloof about him, something so impersonal, so detached. Almost like something frozen, the Lonely Girl thought, as she noted for the thousandth time his steely blue eyes, and his straight, mirthless mouth, and the sprinkling of gray at his temples. Even his voice was like ice; there was an unwilling chill to it.

"I hope," he was saying, "that you'll have a delightful Christmas, every one of you!" Even the warmth of the wish did not quite take the coldness from his voice.

The head stenographer spoke hurriedly. "I'm sure," she said, "that we wish you the same, Mr. Hildreth. And we want to thank you for what we found this morning in our pay envelopes. It was very generous of you."

There, in the doorway, the man seemed to falter. One might almost have suspected him of being embarrassed. Yet why should the giving of extra money at holiday time prove an embarrassment?

"Oh, that's all right, Miss Jamison," he said bruskly. And then, "Merry Christmas!"

"Merry Christmas!" chorused the girls as the plate-glass door swung to behind him. Only one of them had anything further to say.

"I wonder," she said, "if he's like that with the men—the salesmen and the department heads. So far off, I mean?"

One by one they drifted out, like children released from school, each of them with her plans. Only the Lonely Girl, her lips pressed tight together, dawdled at her desk. Only the Lonely Girl, her dark eyes misty with the ache of things, lingered over the washing of her slim hands, the adjusting of her hat. When at last she closed the door of the long room behind her, it was almost one o'clock—almost an hour since the others had left.

With feet that had no need to hurry she went toward the elevator. It did not help to see that the elevator man wore a sprig of holly pinned to the lapel of his coat. Even his cheery greeting did not help. It only emphasized her aloneness—and Christmastime should never be an alone time! She murmured a commonplace answer to his greeting and hurried, rather blindly, toward the street.

The street—and Christmas in the air! Despite the gray sky with the hint of snow in it, despite a dampness in the wind, the Lonely Girl felt the surge of it, the veiled sting. For even as a latent happiness began to grow in her soul, the emptiness of the season—when one hasn't a family—filled her eyes with sudden tears. A stout man with a box that could hold nothing but a doll, a faded woman whose arm was braceleted with wreaths, a group of chattering schoolgirls—all of them belonged to Christmas crowds that pressed by. All of them were going somewhere—and to someone. But she was not going anywhere in particular. Or to anyone. Sharply she swung into the crowd; let it carry her along like a chip upon an ocean. For nearly a block she let it carry her, and then she saw the white restaurant with the glass front.

Perhaps it was because the cook in the window was so round and red that she paused; perhaps because the pancakes he turned had such a golden brown color. Perhaps she hesitated because it was lunchtime, and because being alone does not ease the pangs of hunger. At any rate, she paused.

"I believe," she told herself with a sigh, "I believe I'll go in and have some food. I might as well eat here as anywhere. I might as well——"

From somewhere beside her came a voice, a cheery little voice with a lilt of a reed pipe in it. "Say," said the voice, "don't he turn 'em pretty? Wouldn't you like if you could make some? An' eat a big plate of 'em, after?"

The Lonely Girl looked swiftly away from the red cook. With wide eyes she glanced down at the owner of the voice. She glanced quite far down, for the voice was fastened to a little boy, a very little boy. He too was alone, of all street. The Lonely Girl, seeing the smile in his dark eyes—eyes set staunchly in a wee white face—answered.

"Yes," she said, "I would like to make some. And eat some, too."

The child moved nearer to her with a curiously shuffling movement. It was then that the Lonely Girl noticed, with a sudden stifled cry of pity, the pathetic little crutch that he held under his arm and the cruel twist to his small back. But there was nothing pathetic or cruel about his cheery, piping voice.

"Onct," he told the Lonely Girl, "onct I had pancakes. They was grand. Onct—"

The Lonely Girl was interrupting. "Where," she questioned almost bruskly, to hide the quiver in her voice, "where is your mother, dear? What are you doing here on the street, and all by yourself?"

The child answered slowly. Somehow the lilting note in his voice was blurred, quite as if the reed had been crushed. "I ain't got any mother," he said, "nor father, neither. Mrs. Casey takes care o' me. But it ain't—" quite evidently he was quoting, "like as if I was *her own!*"

Quickly the Lonely Girl changed the subject, almost too quickly. "Do you suppose Mrs. Casey would mind very much," she questioned, "if I should take you into the restaurant with me? Then we could have pancakes together."

The face the little boy lifted to hers was alight with a sudden, incredulous joy. "Honest, do y' want *me?*" he questioned.

The girl nodded. "Honest, I do want you!" she said.

Together they went through the swinging doors, the

girl and the little crippled boy. Together they took their seats opposite each other at a shiny porcelain-topped table. And together they smiled over the spotlessness of it when the order, an order that had to do with many things besides pancakes, had been given.

All about them shoppers with laden arms were hurrying in and out. There was a festive note about them. It was a curiously warming note that caught even at the heart of the little boy.

"Are you goin' t' have a tree," he questioned abruptly, "a tree an' a Santa Claus? Are you?"

The Lonely Girl answered slowly. "I'm afraid not," she told him. "Grown-up people don't have trees."

The child was looking at her with a sudden ache in his great eyes. "Little boys do," he told her. And then, *"Some* little boys!" he amended.

There was silence for a moment, a silence fraught with many meanings. It was the Lonely Girl who broke it.

"It would be nice," she said, and it was as if someone else spoke through her, "it would be nice if the two of us could have a tree—and a Santa Claus—together. Wouldn't it?"

The griddle cakes and the other things had arrived.

But the little boy, being just a bit different from other little boys, did not, at once, begin to eat. "It would be awful nice," he said. "It would be just awful nice. You an' me an' a tree an'—Santa Claus. Only—how'd we be sure t' get Santa Claus t' come? He never come before t' see me—not 'at I can remember!"

Almost desperately the Lonely Girl found herself wishing that she had a brother or a father, someone who would submit to the mock dignity of a white beard and a pillow-stuffed red coat. All at once she began to realize that the plans she had suggested by way of making conversation were becoming almost unbearably real.

"Let's eat our luncheon," she said softly, "and then—"

It was at that moment that, for the second time in an hour, a voice interrupted her. Such a familiar voice it was that the Lonely Girl gazed incredulously up from her plate; such a masculine voice that she dropped a heavy fork with a small clatter upon the marble-topped table. For the voice was one that she had heard perhaps a thousand times. And it was speaking with a curious anxiety in its cool tone.

"Perhaps I can help convince Santa Claus," it said. "Perhaps I can jog his memory!"

The little boy was smiling, friendly-wise, at this helpful stranger. But the Lonely Girl had risen in her place.

"Why, Mr. Hildreth," she gasped, "Mr. Hildreth! How did you happen—"

The man answered. "I saw you with the kiddie, outside," he told her. "I—forgive me—I listened to your conversation. And then I followed you in. And kept on listening. I'm a solitary man, Miss Carleton"—it was the Lonely Girl's name—"and what you were talking about touched a hidden spring somewhere in my heart. Can't we manage somehow to give the little chap a party? Can't we?"

As if in a dream the Lonely Girl heard herself answering. "I live in a small apartment uptown," she said. "We could have a tree there."

The little boy, his cheeks bulging with griddle cakes, interrupted. "D' you mean it?" his reed voice questioned. *"You ain't kidding me?"*

It was the man who answered. "No, we're not kidding you," he said. And then, "I live alone myself, Miss Carleton. I have no kin. Christmas is a rather desperate time for a man with no kin. If we three can get together—" he hesitated. "Well, it won't do any harm! And it may help us all tremendously."

"But"—the question came unwillingly to the girl's lips—"but what would they think at the office—if they knew?"

All at once the man's eyes were boyishly appealing.

One almost forgot the frost-like gray at his temples. "I don't give a hang for what they'd think!" he said. "Do you?"

"No, I don't," murmured the Lonely Girl.

For a moment she was near to forgetting the little boy.

After luncheon—an unbelievably jolly luncheon—they left the white restaurant and went out again to the street. Strangely enough, it had ceased to be a torment, that street. Or else it was that they had ceased to be apart from it—maybe it was because they had become, in some curious fashion—related to it! As the Lonely Girl helped the little boy into a certain big car drawn up to the curb, she felt like Cinderella. And as the man took his place at the steering wheel and started to weave his way through the traffic, the little boy had almost the same sort of feeling.

"It's like magic, ain't it?" said the little boy.

First of all they found Mrs. Casey in a tenement room with little air and less light. A ten-dollar bill made Mrs. Casey happy and more than reconciled to parting, for a day, with the little boy.

"A crippled kid," she said bluntly, "is a pest. I'd 'a put him in an orphanage, only his mother was my second cousin, an' I give her a promise that he'd always have a good home. Nobody'd want to adopt a cripple—not when th' 'sylums is full of healthy kids. Not—" speaking as one who gives credit where it is due, "not that Benny ain't a good boy. He is that. But he ain't much use."

With quick tears in her eyes the Lonely Girl hurried the little boy from the room. The man—who had once seemed frozen—came more slowly behind them. Perhaps there were tears in his eyes, too. But his voice was cheery, and his touch was very tender as he lifted the child again into the car.

"Where to, now?" he questioned.

The Lonely Girl spoke. "Suppose we go after our tree," she said. *"Our tree!"*

Again through the streets they whirled—the streets with Christmas in the very fabric of them. The little boy sat silently, with wide eyes, and one hand clasped in the Lonely Girl's hand. And the Lonely Girl was silent, too. Only the man was not silent; he was whistling, softly and content-edly, half to himself.

In front of the largest florist shop they stopped—it was to be no cheap affair, this tree! They stopped, and the man lifted the little boy down. And they went together into the place of fragrance and growing things.

❖

It might have been an enchanted forest that they went into, this largest florist shop, on the day before Christmas. Orchids and roses and lilies-of-the-valley! Violets, in great April clusters, and lilacs mistily sweet. Poinsettias, fairly shouting the joy of the season, and mistletoe. And back of everything the trees, spicily fragrant and thrillingly green. Back of everything—the trees!

Of course, the man wanted the largest tree. He had always wanted the best—and he had usually been able to get it; that was why his name was printed in letters of gold upon the door of a private office. He spoke authoritatively to a clerk, while the girl nodded dreamily in the background and the little boy—almost red-cheeked with eagerness—hopped up and down on his crutch. And then began the work of selection.

They touched the trees gently. This one was larger than the others—yes. But this one was almost feathery with needles, and its branches were unbelievably regular. The man and the girl, almost breathlessly eager, followed the clerk, and the little boy poked into the dimmest corners. It was his voice, suddenly, that made them pause in the work of choosing.

"I like this one," said the little boy, his wee face peering gnomelike from between two branches. "This one!"

After all, Christmas trees were for children. In nearly

227

shamefaced manner the man and the girl turned toward the little boy.

"Which one, dear?" questioned the girl.

There was something affectionate in the way that the child's hand rested upon the twisted trunk of the smallest tree. There was a spirit of brotherhood in the touch of his thin fingers that made one notice acutely the tree's aching deficiencies. For it was a stunted tree, a bent tree, a tree that through some pitiful freak of nature had grown crooked.

There was annoyance in the clerk's voice as he spoke. "That tree," he told the man, quite ignoring the little boy, "was sent to us by mistake. It was never meant for a Christmas tree! We can only sell the best here. The very best."

For one moment the man hesitated; it was such a mean sort of broken thing. And then he turned appealingly to the girl.

"Why," he questioned, "has he chosen *that?*" A jerk of his thumb indicated the tree that had been sent by mistake.

The girl did not answer, but her heart was shining from her eyes as she went toward the little boy. She was near to understanding.

"Are you sure, dear," she questioned, "that you like that tree best?"

The little boy's voice was positive, quite positive. His

228

cheeks were still red. "It's a cripple tree," he told the girl. "It ain't like—th' other trees. Nobody'd want it—ever—but us. It'd just get left, always. An' never trimmed with tinsel an' lights, like th' rest o' the trees'll be trimmed. I guess it's pretty lonely for a tree that's crooked, when all th' rest of th' trees are straight!"

Even the clerk had no further objection to offer.

They took the tree home to the girl's apartment. On the way to the apartment they paused at sundry thrilling stores for silver ornaments and gold ones, and tiny electric bulbs in the shape of singing birds. Crepe paper they bought, and garlands of ground pine, and a huge knot of mistletoe. The motor car was like Santa's own sleigh when it stopped, finally, at its destination.

As they went up the three flights to her rooms, the man going first with the little boy upon his broad shoulders, the Lonely Girl experienced a curious feeling of unreality. She found herself wondering, suddenly, what the head stenographer would think if she could glance in, for a moment, upon their ascending backs.

As she fitted her key into a lock, she wondered what the blonde girl would say. But strangely enough, as the door swung open, it was of the girl who had talked of going home that she thought. Suddenly she was remembering how the word "home" had hurt, a few hours before. And all at once she was conscious that the word had stopped hurting. For the apartment was no longer an empty shell of a place to her. It was something brighter and better now. A child's laugh had worked the miracle; a man's step in her tiny living room had done magic things!

They propped the little boy up against cushions on the shabby sofa—not that they expected him to stay there. And then, after several trips down the three flights, they were ready.

Against a background of Christmas greens they set up the little twisted tree. It didn't look quite so crooked against the friendliness of that background. The girl's hand, slipping along one of the bent branches, brushed, quite by accident, against the man's hand. And they both smiled, almost shyly.

The little boy was exuberant. You see, it was his party! With wide eyes that held no shadow of wistfulness he directed operations. "I'd put a red ball there," he'd say, and then, "How 'bout a strip o' tinsel in that bare place?"

And every once in a while he'd cuddle up close to one of his newfound friends, and his whisper of joy would be almost piercingly sweet.

"It looks awful happy, the tree!" he'd whisper. "It looks awful happy—don't it?"

The situation—to the head stenographer—might have seemed unconventional. Under ordinary circumstances it would certainly have seemed more than unconventional to both the girl and the man. But conventions don't stand for much on the day before Christmas! As they worked together, laughing and joking, the Lonely Girl's prim hair spun itself into tiny curls across her forehead, and her eyes danced. And like a cloak the coldness slipped from the man who had also been lonely. They fell to talking, quite naturally, about the little intimate things of life that weren't very important and yet mattered infinitely much!

It wasn't strange that, along about teatime—when the shadows were just beginning to quiver over the floor—the little boy should fall suddenly asleep against the softness of the cushions. He wasn't used, you see, to so much excitement. It was then that the man and the girl, having covered him with a shawl, realized that they too were tired. And so the girl lighted a bayberry candle, and they sat down in the dusk together. And it was Christmas Eve!

"You know"—it was the man who spoke first—"you know, Miss Carleton, you've given me a great deal of pleasure today. Just letting me help." He paused, and his voice quivered ever so slightly. *"It's been a long time since my soul has kept holiday!"*

The Lonely Girl—quite without meaning to—rested her fingers for a moment on the rough tweed of his coat sleeve. All at once words came fairly tumbling over each other, from her very heart. "It's hard, of course," she said, "for a man to be by himself in a huge city. But it's harder for a girl. I was used to a home, you see, and a mother. And—ever so long ago—a father. I used to hang up my stocking, and we had carols early Christmas morning. And there was turkey and plum pudding for dinner. I—I've missed it"—her voice faltered—"and today I was missing it more than ever, I think. If it hadn't been for the kiddie"—her gaze rested softly upon the little boy—"I would have been crying, this minute, with my head in a pillow!"

The man's voice was filled with a deep understanding. "I know," he said. "I'd not have been crying—but I know. People need company—and kiddies—at Christmastime. *And at every time.*"

There was a tremor in his tone that made the girl change the subject just a bit hurriedly.

"How," she questioned, "shall we manage a Santa Claus? We promised one, you know!"

The man was all enthusiasm. Had he ever really been a cool and detached person? "I've often thought that I'd like to play Santa to children of my own," he said, "and this youngster will be a mighty good substitute, bless him! See here—this is what we'll do: I'll take you all out to dinner. And I'll leave with a bunch of dandy excuses—about ice cream time. I'll stop at a costumer's, and when you get back, Santa'll be here waiting."

There was a ring of youth—youth eternal—in his voice. And there was something else. It was the something else that made the girl cross the room suddenly to the sofa upon which the little boy was so peacefully sleeping.

"I wonder," she said slowly, "if you would stop at Mrs. Casey's and tell her that I'm keeping Benny overnight. Somehow I can't bear to let him go—before Christmas really comes!" She bent swiftly and kissed the child's flushed cheek.

They got to the first-name stage at the dinner table. The man's first name was Jim. And the Lonely Girl admitted to Nancy. She also admitted to other things.

"Do you know," she said, "that I thought you were a crabby old thing, once?"

"Do you know," the man answered, "that I never knew you were beautiful until this afternoon?"

At ice cream time the party slowed up, just a bit, for

the man left. But the little boy and the Lonely Girl had a wonderful white dessert with candied cherries set in stars around the top. And when it had all been devoured, as such desserts should be, they went back to the apartment. And a stout red and white Santa Claus—rather like a dessert himself—opened the door. And the little boy screamed with an excited indrawing of the breath, just as little boys and some grown-ups scream when a skyrocket goes up into the air.

There were gifts everywhere. It was as if the lonely, twisted tree had, in gratitude, blossomed. There were gifts that were sensible, such as shoes and mittens, and gifts that were utterly frivolous—such as mechanical toys and American Beauty roses. There was a marvelous electric train that wound on tracks all over the living room. It was while the girl and the little boy were busy adjusting the tracks of it that Santa Claus disappeared with never a word of farewell. And when, a few moments later, the man sauntered in, it was to find a little boy sobbing in the arms of a gloriously disheveled girl-woman.

"He lef'," the little boy was moaning, "an' I never told him what I wanted *most!*"

The girl was pressing the tired little head to her shoulder. "Why, honey," she sympathized, "I didn't know that there was anything else that you really wanted! Tell Nancy!"

The little boy's arms were flung suddenly around her neck. "I want *folks*," sobbed the little boy, "of my own. Folks 'at won't mind because my back ain't straight. Folks 'at'll love me—like I love my tree—an' not care!"

The man was leaning over the two of them. "I don't blame you, old fellow," he said, "for wanting folks. I want them myself. Santa Claus didn't bring me anything really important, either. He came when I was away. So you and I are in the same boat."

The crying of the little boy in no way diminished. His voice came up from the girl's shoulder in a muffled way.

"But you got each other!" he choked.

Suddenly, and with no idea at all of dramatics, the man was down on his knees in a clutter of tracks, beside them. Suddenly his arms were around them both.

"Oh, Nancy, have we?" he choked. "Have we got—each other?"

There was a glow in the girl's eyes—the glow that once looked out of the first woman's eyes in a garden place. But her words were of the child, when she spoke.

"Do you think that she'd let *us* have him?" she questioned, and she moved closer into his arms as she spoke. "Mrs. Casey, I mean?"

All at once the man was sobbing, himself. But the little boy was suddenly quiet, radiantly quiet.

235

In the corner the little lonely tree—lonely no longer—stood beaming proudly down upon them. Every colorful glass ball, every bird-shaped electric light, was like a separate chuckle. One, looking at it as it stood there, could hardly notice that it wasn't quite—straight.

A Few Bars in the Key of G

✤

CLIFTON CARLISLE
OSBORNE

Probably my favorite of all Christmas stories set in the Old West is this one. The reader is carried along pell-mell with the O'Henry-ish narrative, not knowing until the very end what in the world is really going on.

No story in my collection of Christmas stories has been greeted with more joy and gratitude than this one. Many had heard it once or twice in their youth, then spent the rest of their lives trying to find it again. Seemingly, it had disappeared off the face of the earth. We include it here for a whole new generation to enjoy.

One of the most exciting events of the past few years for me was the arrival of a small tan package from my good friend Jean Krenrich of Deltona, Florida. In it was a rather dim transcript of "A Few Bars in the Key of G." I did a double-take as I discovered, for the first time, the identity of the story's author. The transcript also supplied several missing pieces of the story puzzle—even providing entire new scenes!

Strangely enough, however, both versions proved to be incomplete and flawed, each providing portions the other missed. In the end, I interwove the texts, retaining the best lines from each version. Thus the following text is quite probably the most complete, and most moving, since the publication of the original text around a century ago.

It was two o'clock and time for the third watch on the night herd. These two facts gradually impressed themselves on the consciousness of John Talbot Waring as he was thumped into wakefulness by the Mexican "house wrangler."

He sat up and sleepily groped for his boots; unrolled his slicker, which had been serving as a pillow, enveloped himself in its clammy folds, and went out into the drizzling rain.

There was a moon above the heavy clouds, but it might as well have been on the other side of the earth for all the assistance it gave in the operation of saddling two of the picketed horses. The herd lay to the north of the camp, and settling reluctantly into their seats, the drowsy riders turned their horses in that direction, trusting to the instinct of the animals to find the herd. The darkness was intense, and the wiry little beasts were obliged to pick their way cautiously.

Approaching carefully, to avoid startling the cattle, the two riders separated, and relieving the tired watchers, they commenced the three hours' vigil, one going on the opposite side of the herd. The cattle were unusually quiet, needing little attention, thus Waring had ample opportunity to reflect on the disadvantages of a cowpuncher's life as he rode slowly along the edge of the black mass of sleeping animals. The rain dripped from the limp brim of his sombrero and ran in little streams down his slicker into his already soaking boots. The chill wind, sweeping down from the mountains, pierced his damp clothing and made him shiver in the saddle. For the hundredth time within a week,

Waring condemned himself for relinquishing the comforts of civilization for this hard life, riding these rough and dangerous slopes of Colorado.

He recalled his arrival on the range six months before, a tenderfoot; the various tribulations he had endured incident to his transformation into a full-fledged cowpuncher. Of the hardships and dangers that come to every rider of the range, he had experienced his share and faced them bravely, thereby winning the respect of the rough, lion-hearted men among whom he had cast his lot.

But all the weary months had been wasted; he had failed in his object—he could not forget. He was not the first to learn that one cannot escape memory by merely crossing the continent. It seemed to him that instead of growing more endurable with time, the soreness of his heart and the sting of regret increased with each passing day. He wondered if *she* felt the separation; if *she* cared. As his thoughts wandered back over the past two years, he recalled every incident of their acquaintance as distinctly as though it occurred but yesterday. The day he had first seen her as she stepped gracefully out beside the piano to sing at a musical he had attended.

The hours I spent with thee, dear heart,
Are as a string of pearls to me.

The sweet days which followed——their enjoyment together of symphony, oratorio, and opera; for both being amateurs of no mean ability, they had met and loved upon the common ground of their love of divine harmony.

He looked into the blackness of the night, and could see her as she appeared on that wonderful day when he had met her at the altar of Trinity Church, and spoken the words that were to bind them together through life. How beautiful she was. He looked back at their wedding trip as a dream. How well he remembered their return to the lovely home he had prepared for her. How happy they had been, and how he had loved her. *Had* loved her? He *did* love her. That was his sorrow. He realized now that as long as he had life, his whole heart would be hers alone.

And then the shadow had come over their home. He asked himself bitterly why he had not been more patient with her and made allowance for her high spirits and quick temper. She was such a child. He could see now that he had been to blame many times in their quarrels, when at the time he had sincerely believed himself in the right. Should he go back to her and admit that he was in the wrong? Never! The memory of that last day was too clear in his mind. The words she had spoken in the heat of her anger had burned themselves into his soul and could not be for-

gotten. He wondered now that he had been so calm. He recalled every word he had said:

"Your words convince me that we cannot live together any longer. I will neither forgive nor forget them. I
am going away. You are at liberty to sue for divorce, if you
care to do so. Three years, I believe, is the time required to
substantiate a plea for desertion." That was all. Without a
word he had left her, standing white and motionless in the
center of her dainty chamber, and gone from the beautiful
home in white-hot rage, to come out here to the wildest
spot he could find in the vain effort to forget.

He pulled down the dripping brim of his sombrero to
shelter his face from the wind, then turned his thoughts in
other directions. He thought of his friends at the clubs—
did they miss him? From them his thoughts strayed to the
strange postal card he had received the previous day, and he
began to puzzle his brain in the effort to decide who had
sent it and what it could mean. It had been directed to his
lawyer and forwarded to the remote mountain post office
where Waring received his mail. It was an ordinary postal
card, its peculiarity consisting in the fact that the communication on the back was composed, not in words, but music—*four measures in the key of G.*

He had hummed the notes over and over and thought
they had a strangely familiar sound, yet he could not place

the fragment, nor even the composer. It had a meaning, of that he was convinced, but what could it be? Who could have sent it? Among his friends were many musicians, any one of them might have adopted such a method of communication with him. He began to hum the phrase as he rode round and round the cattle.

After a while, Waring abandoned the riddle of the postal card, began to sing to pass the time, and his rich baritone rang out above the sleeping herd. The light slowly appeared above the peaks. One by one the cattle stirred, rose, and commenced to graze. Waring still sang, carelessly passing from snatches of opera to lines of sacred harmony. Suddenly, while in the midst of a passage from one of the great works of a master composer, he stopped short in surprise: *he was singing the notes on the card!* It had come to him like a flash. He tore his coat open and drew the postal card from the inner pocket. There was no mistake. Almost mechanically he reached for a pencil and *wrote the words* under the lines of music, added a signature, and gazed long and earnestly; then, with a wild shout, he wheeled and rode furiously to camp.

Pulling up with a jerk that almost lifted the iron-jawed bronco from the ground, he literally hurled himself from the saddle and reached the boss in two bounds.

"I must be in Denver tonight! I want your best horse quick!"

The boss stared at him in astonishment. "Why, man, it's a hundred and twenty miles. You're crazy!"

Waring fairly stamped with impatience. "It's only sixty to Empire, and I can get the train there. It leaves at one o'clock, and I can make it if you will lend me Star! I know he's your pet horse, and you never let anyone else ride him, but I simply must get there."

Coberly scowled. "You ought to know, Jack, that I won't loan Star. None of the other horses can get over there in that time, so you might just as well give up. What's the matter with you . . . that you're in such a confounded rush?"

Waring thought a moment, and then drawing the boss beyond earshot of the listening cowpunchers, spoke to him rapidly and earnestly, finally handing him the postal card. Coberly scanned it intensely, and a change came over his face.

"Why didn't you show me this first? Of course you can have the horse. . . . Hi, there! Some of you boys round up the horses and rope Star for Mr. Waring. Jump lively!"

The men made a mad rush for their saddles, and in an incredibly short time several of them were racing across the plain in the direction of the horses. Waring dove into his tent and began gathering his few possessions while Coberly plunged around outside, giving orders at the top of his voice.

"Roll up some grub for Mr. Waring, quick. Nick, you get his canteen an' fill it out of my jug. Fly around now!"

A rush of hoofs announced the arrival of the horse and his escort, just as Waring emerged from the tent with his little bundle. A dozen hands made quick work of saddling, and with a hurried goodbye, he swung himself astride the magnificent animal and was off on his long ride. He looked back and saw the boys in a group around the boss, who was explaining the cause of his hasty departure. Presently a tremendous yell reached his ears, and he saw hats exuberantly thrown high into the air. He waved his hand in reply and settled down in his saddle.

The long pacing stride of Coberly's pet covered the ground in a surprising manner, and eight o'clock found twenty-three miles behind his nimble feet. It lacked twenty minutes of ten o'clock when Waring drew rein. He unsaddled and turned the thoroughbred into a trailside corral. A half hour's rest would put new life into him. Yet, it was still twenty miles to the railroad, and only three hours in which to cover it. It seemed impossible.

A quarter past ten, Star, refreshed by an energetic rubbing and a mouthful of water, was carrying him up the road with no apparent loss of power. Up, up they went, mile after mile, until the plain they had left was spreading out like a map behind them. Two miles from the top, Waring dismounted and led his panting horse along the icy trail. The rarefied air seemed to burn his lungs as he struggled the remaining distance to the summit of the pass, twelve thousand feet above the sea.

Twelve o'clock. He stopped and anxiously examined the horse that had carried him so well. The inspection reassured him. There was plenty of life and energy left in Star yet. One hour, and twelve miles to go—could he make it? He must! A final pull at the cinches and Waring was again in the saddle, racing down the steep and dangerous path toward the sea of dark green forest that stretched far below.

Down the long slopes, around dizzy curves, slipping, swaying, followed by loose stones and gravel, they went faster than ever that trail was covered before. Star swung into a strong lope and his rider drew a long breath. Not till then did he realize the strain of that wild ride. Rounding a turn in the road, he spied a horseman approaching and turned out to pass him. The stranger eyed him sharply as he drew near and suddenly slipped out a six-shooter!

"Hold up there! I want to talk to you!"

For a moment Waring considered the chance of riding over the man, but for a moment only. The stranger

248

looked too determined, and his aim was sure. He pulled up, raging. "I suppose you want my money," he snarled. "Well, you're welcome to it if you'll leave me enough to pay my fare to Denver."

"That's a good bluff, but it won't do. I'm the sheriff, an' I want to know where you're going running off with Joe Coberly's horse?"

"Oh, is that all you want? Why, I've been working for Coberly and he lent me the horse to ride over to catch the train." And he gathered up his reins to ride on.

"Hold on, young man!" commanded the sheriff, as he raised his gun suggestively. "That yarn won't hold water. I know old Joe, and I happen to know that he wouldn't a lent that horse to his own brother, let alone one of his cow-punchers. I guess I'll have to lock you up till the boys come over after you."

Waring groaned. "Look here, Mr. Sheriff, I'm telling you the truth. Coberly let me take the horse because it was the only one that could get me over here in time to catch the train, and I had to be in Denver tonight, without fail."

His captor shook his head. "It's no use, my friend, your story won't hold. Why are you in such a tearin' hurry, anyway?"

Waring remembered the postal; he reached into his breast pocket and produced it. "Here, sir, that is my reason for haste . . . and that is why Coberly let me take his horse."

Keeping his captive covered with the muzzle of his revolver, the officer rode closer and took the card. As he read it, his face lighted up and he lowered his gun. "That's all right, youngster. I'm sorry I stopped you. I don't wonder Joe lent you the horse. I hope you won't miss the train. I'll ride down on account of the horse—everybody knows him."

Waring touched Star with his spur and rode forward, with the repentant sheriff by his side. Just over the rise they could see the town before them, about a mile distant. The train was already at the station! Another touch of the spur and Star stretched out in a run that gradually left the sheriff behind. A half mile yet to go—a quarter—the black smoke began to come in puffs from the funnel of the engine, and a line of cars moved slowly away from the station. Then it was that Star showed the spirit that was in him. He bounded forward and swept down upon the town like a whirlwind.

As the usual crowd of train-time loafers lounged around the station, their attention was caught by the two swiftly approaching riders, and they paused to watch the race. Presently one cried, "Hullow, the first horse is Coberly's black—an' he sure is movin'. Why the other fellow is the sheriff! An' he's after him. Horse thief!"

The others took up the cry of "Horse thief!" Thus

when Waring flashed past them at Star's top speed, a volley of shots greeted him. Fortunately the bullets went wild, and before any more could be fired the sheriff tore into the crowd and roared, "Stop that shootin'! That man's all right. He's only trying to catch the train!" Then there was a mad rush to the track, where a view of the race could be obtained.

The road ran for a mile beside the track as level as a floor. The train was gathering speed with every revolution of the wheels, but Star was traveling fast too and gaining at every jump. The crowd at the station danced and howled in their excitement: "Will he make it?" "He's gaining!" "Look at that horse go!" "Hooray for the Black!" "He'll make it! He'll make it!"

Waring, with eyes fixed and jaw set, was riding desperately. Thirty feet—the spectators in the doorway of the last car gazed breathlessly. Twenty feet—and Star straining every nerve and muscle in his body. Ten feet, and still he gained. Only five feet now. Inch by inch, he crawled up! He was abreast of the platform! Swerving his flying horse close to the track, Waring leaned over and, grasping the railings with both hands, lifted himself free from the saddle, kicked his feet free from the stirrups, and swung himself over to the step of the car. The faint sound of a cheer reached him from the distant station.

✤

After calmly accepting the enthusiastic congratulations of the passengers who had witnessed his dramatic boarding of the train, Waring dropped into a seat with a sigh of relief and was soon lost in thought. He was roused from his revery by a touch on his arm and turned to find the conductor standing beside him. The sight reminding him of the necessity of paying his fare, he reached into his pocket for the required cash. His fingers encountered nothing more valuable than a knife and some matches. Then, with a shock, he remembered: he had put all his money in that little bundle, at that moment firmly attached to the saddle, miles to the rear!

There was nothing to do but throw himself on the mercy of the man in the blue uniform. Leaning over, he whispered something in the conductor's ear and ended by showing him the now precious card. The conductor was suspicious, but a glance at Waring's earnest face reassured him. His expression softened. "I reckon I'll have to fix it for you, but the only way I can do it is to pay your fare out of my own pocket. It's $3.60. You can send me the money." This occurrence reminded Waring of a similar difficulty to be overcome in Denver. But . . . the card had served him well thus far . . . perhaps its mission was not yet ended.

Arriving at the station, he quickly disembarked and

searched for a carriage. Finding one, he was driven quickly to the nearest drugstore, where he consulted a directory.

"To 900 South Seventeenth Street," he cried as he entered the vehicle. Arriving at his destination, he sprang out and, saying "Wait," ran up the steps of the palatial residence.

To the dignified butler who opened the door, he said, "I wish to see Mr. Foster. My name is Waring, and I haven't a card with me."

That gentleman entered almost immediately. "What can I do for you, Mr. Waring?" asked the man of finance.

"Mr. Foster, you are the president of the Denver National Bank, which I believe handles the Western interests of the Second National Bank of Boston?"

"Yes."

"I have an account at the Second, and I want you to cash a check for me. It is after banking hours, I know; and even if it were not I have no immediate means of identification. It is of the greatest importance that I take the Eastern Express tonight, or I would not have come to you in this irregular way—"

"One moment, Mr. Waring. Pardon me for interrupting you, but it will save your time as well as mine if I say that what you ask is impossible, as you should know. My advice to you is to wire your bank for the money."

"Of course I know that I can do that, but it means a

day's delay, and that is what I want to avoid. See here, Mr. Foster, I am willing to pay any amount within reason for the accommodation, if you will oblige me."

"It must be a very urgent matter that requires such haste. Really, Mr. Waring, I must positively decline to do anything for you."

"It *is* an urgent matter!" And he told of the postal card and its purpose, adding a brief account of his efforts to get to the city in time to take the train that night.

"Let me see the card. From what is it taken, did you say?"

Upon hearing the answer, he left the room to return in a few minutes with a rather bulky musical score, which he laid upon the table, then turned the pages until he found what he sought. Carefully he compared the music on the card with that on the printed sheet. Then, turning to the younger man, he said in a kindly voice:

"I will assist you, Mr. Waring. I am a rather good judge of faces and feel safe in trusting you. It will, of course, be purely a personal matter, as it is contrary to all my business methods, but I cannot resist such an appeal as this. What amount do you require?"

"One hundred dollars will serve my purpose."

"Make your check out for one hundred and fifty. You will need that much unless you care to travel in your present costume. You can cash this at the Brown Palace Hotel. I will phone the cashier, so you will have no trouble."

Waring tried to thank him, but he would not listen.

"You are perfectly welcome, my boy. I am glad to be able to help you. You have my best wishes for a pleasant journey. Goodbye."

A swift handclasp and Waring was running down the steps to the carriage.

"Telegraph office!" he shouted.

Ten minutes later, these words were speeding over the wire: POSTAL RECEIVED. ARRIVE BOSTON FRIDAY NIGHT. SEE LUKE 1:13—JACK.

When the Chicago Limited pulled out of Denver that evening, John Talbot Waring, clean-shaven and attired in garments of the most approved fashion, was standing on the rear platform of the last Pullman, softly humming a passage from the great oratorio *The Messiah*. There was a tender light in his eyes as he gazed at the postal card he held in his hand. And these were the words he read:

> For unto us a child is born;
> Unto us a son is given.

At the same moment, two thousand miles away in the East, a pale young wife was holding a telegram close to her lips. An open Bible lay on the bed beside her. Turning softly on her pillows, she glanced lovingly at the dainty cradle and whispered:

"Thou shalt call his name, John."

The Snow
of Christmas

�֍

JOE WHEELER

*How is a story born? I don't know; it just
comes to you. One bitterly cold December
evening in 1989, when I had just turned
in grades for my creative writing class, the
mood came upon me to write a Christmas
story of my own.*

*Misunderstandings—every mar-
riage is full of them. But what happens
when they are permitted to grow
unchecked? What then? We all know the*

answer: another divorce. As I looked out at the snow and ice on the river, and heard the cold wind shriek as it savaged the trees, there was born the story of a great love destroyed by a quarrel.

I sent out copies to friends. So many wrote back, thanking me and encouraging me to print it, that it proved to be a catalyst for putting the first Christmas in My Heart *collection together.*

John, Cathy, and Julie—and then there were only two.

Three doors he had slammed on her: the bedroom, the front, and the car. What started it all, he really couldn't say; it was just one of those misunderstandings that grow into quarrels. In a matter of minutes he had unraveled a relationship that had taken years to build. His tongue, out of control, appeared to have a life of its own, divorced as it was from his accusing mind and withdrawing heart.

"Catherine . . . It's all been a big mistake . . . you and me. I've tried and tried—Heaven knows I've tried—but it just won't work. You're . . . you're wrong for me . . . and I'm wrong for you."

"John!"

"Don't interrupt me. I mean it. We're through. What

we thought was love, wasn't. It just wasn't . . . No sense in prolonging a dead thing. Don't worry, I'll see to it that you don't suffer financially—I'll keep making the house payments. . . . And uh . . . and uh, you can keep what's in the checking and savings accounts. . . . And uh, uh, don't worry, I'll send child support for Julie!"

"John!"

Almost, he came to his senses as he looked into Catherine's anguished eyes and saw the shock and the tears. But his pride was at stake; ignoring the wounded appeal of those azure eyes, he had stormed out, his leaving punctuated by the three slammed doors.

Three weeks later, here he was, pacing a lonely motel room three thousand miles from home. Home? He had no home. He had only his job—a very good one—and his Mercedes. That was all.

Unable to face the prosecuting attorney of his mind, he turned on the TV, but that didn't help much. There were Christmas-related commercials or programs on every channel—one of these ads featured a golden-haired little girl who reminded him far too much of Julie.

He remembered Julie's wide-eyed anticipation of every Christmas. The presents under the tree that she'd surreptitiously pick up and evaluate by weight and size and sound, and the finesse with which she unwrapped and

❖

rewrapped them . . . ; he found it hard to be stern with her for did not Catherine too unwrap them on the sly? It seemed that Catherine had been constitutionally unable to wait until Christmas should reveal what hid within gaily-wrapped packages bearing her name, so poor Julie came about this affliction naturally.

Again, he switched channels. Wouldn't you know it—yet another Christmas special. Had to be Perry Como . . . *Still* at it. Why, the Christmas special advertised as Como's farewell performance was a number of years back—in fact, he and Catherine heard it the Christmas season of Julie's birth . . . Como no longer had the range, but his middle tones still carried him through.

Oh no! Not "I'll Be Home for Christmas" . . . "you can plan on me . . ." On the wings of Como's voice he soared backward in time, all the way back to his own childhood.

Was it his seventh Christmas, or his eighth? "The eighth!" . . . for that was the year his parents had surprised him with an adorable shaded-silver Persian kitten, which he promptly named Samantha. Samantha had lived a long time—fifteen years, in fact. It was hard to envision life without that bundle of purring fur that cuddled up next to his feet every night until he left for college. And even then, whenever he returned home, every night, like clockwork, within sixty seconds from when he turned out the light and slipped into bed, he would sense a slight vibration resulting from a four-point landing; he would hear a loud purr, and feel a whiskered head searching for a head-scratching.

Memories flooded in upon him in torrents now. How he had loved Christmas at home. His had always been the responsibility of decorating the Christmas tree—a tree he got to pick out himself. A *real* tree, never a fake! The fragrance of a real tree, the sticky feel of a real tree, even the shedding of a real tree, were all intertwined in the memories of the years.

Strange . . . passing strange . . . how he measured the years by specific Christmases.

The Christmas of the "Broken Phonograph Records," with its now legendary "lean-to" by . . . uh . . . Mari Sandoz—yeah, Sandoz wrote it. How everyone had laughed and cried over that Nebraska frontier tale. "Lean-to" had gone into the family lexicon of memories. And, as usual, all four of his grandparents had been there, and numerous aunts, uncles, cousins, and family friends.

Then there was the Christmas when Dad, for the first time, read *all* of Dickens's "A Christmas Carol"—he had thought it would never end. But strangely, ever since that first reading, the story of Scrooge and the Cratchits seemed shorter every time it was read. And theater and movie renditions? They but reinforced the impact of the core story.

And how could he ever forget the first time he had heard Henry Van Dyke's "The Other Wise Man"? Like Dickens's tale, it normally took several evenings to read. That poignant conclusion where the dying Artaban, under the extended shadow of Golgotha, at last finds his king—it never failed to bring tears to his eyes.

"That's *enough,* John! You've got to put all that behind you. Christmas? What is it but Madison Avenue's annual process of grafting sales to sentiment? That's why the first Christmas sale now takes place the day after Independence Day." But it wasn't enough: he just could not convince himself that Christmas meant no more than that. Instead, his mind flung open a door and replayed the scene in his parents' kitchen three weeks before.

It had been anything but easy—rather, it had been perhaps the hardest thing he had ever done, telling them about the separation and impending divorce. And he had begged off from being home for this Christmas, telling them that a very important business meeting on the East Coast would make it impossible.

Mother had broken down when she heard about the end of his marriage, for Catherine had slipped into their hearts, becoming the daughter they had always yearned for, that first Christmas when he brought her home from college. Catherine had taken it all in: the warmth and radiance of the *real* tree; the crudely carved nativity scene (John had made it when he was twelve); the exterior Christmas lights; the Christmas decorations everywhere; the Christmas music played on the stereo and sung around the piano; the Christmas stories read during the week; the puns, jokes, kidding, and ever-present laughter; the crazy annual trading game—which was more fun than the usual exchange of presents; the bounteous table groaning with delicious food day after day; parlor games such as Monopoly, caroms, dominoes, anagrams; the crackling fire every evening; the remembering of the Christ Child; and the warmth and love that permeated every corner of the modest home.

When he had proposed—on Christmas Eve—and apologized for the plainness of the home, and compared it to the Marin County estate where she grew up, her eyes had blazed and she had hushed his lips with her fingers.

"Don't you *ever* apologize for your home, John!" she exclaimed. "There is *love* here, and Christ, and Father, *and* Mother—not just my lonely embittered father rattling around in all those endless rooms, *alone*. No, this"—she paused as her gaze took it all in again—"this is the kind of home I've longed for all my life." Then her eyes, reflecting the firelight glow, softened and emanated such tender, trusting love—unqualified and unreserved—that time stopped for him as he gathered into his arms what had once seemed virtually unattainable.

"This has got to stop!" he admonished himself. "There can be no turning back!" Out of the room he strode, down the hall, down the stairs, and out into the city. The streets were crowded with people—it was December 23—all with one goal: get those last-minute gifts. He passed two Salvation Army bell ringers, and left a five-dollar bill with each one.

Happiness and seasonal good humor were all around him. Strangers wished him a very merry Christmas. Christmas carols were piped into almost every store.

His attention was caught by a crowd in front of Macy's biggest window; he pushed himself far enough in to be able to see what they were all looking at. What he saw, in a fairyland setting, were hundreds of cashmere teddy bears in varying costumes. Julie had fallen in love with them the first time she saw them (long before they had become the rage of the season). And he had planned to surprise her on Christmas morning by bringing it to her at the breakfast table rather than putting it under the tree. Oh well, perhaps Catherine would remember to buy it, that is—which he rather doubted—if she was in the mood to have Christmas at all.

He moved on, but seemed to feel an invisible force pulling him back to Macy's. Two hours later, unable to resist any longer, he went back, bought one of the last three in stock—even the window had been cleaned out—and returned to the motel. He shook his head, not understanding in the least why he had bought it, for he was a continent away from Julie—and tomorrow was Christmas Eve.

After depositing the teddy bear in his room, he returned to the street. This time, he walked away from the downtown district. He came to a large white New England-style church. The front doors were open, and floating out on the night air were the celestial strains of "Ave Maria." He stopped, transfixed; then he walked up the steps and into the church. There, down candlelit aisles, at the front of the church, was a live nativity scene. Off to the side, a lovely brunette, eyes luminous with the illusion of the moment, was singing the same song he had first heard Catherine sing, and with the same intensity, forgetfulness of self, and sincerity.

When she reached those last few measures and her pure voice seemed to commingle with the angels, chills went up and down his spine; when the last note died away into infinity, there came the ultimate accolade of total silence . . . followed by a storm of applause.

John closed his eyes, soothed yet tormented by what he had just experienced, by whom the singer reminded him of, and by the significance of that mother's love and sacrifice two thousand years ago.

Out of the sanctuary he strode, and down the street, mile after mile, until he had left even the residential district behind. On and on he walked; he did not stop until the city lights no longer kept him from seeing the stars. As he looked up into the cold December sky, for the first time in three traumatic weeks he faced his inner self.

And he did not like what he saw.

Etched for all time in the grooves of his memory were the terrible words he had spoken to the woman he had pledged his life to. How could he have been so cruel— even if he no longer loved her? That brought him face-to-face with the rest of his life. The question, the answer, and what he would do about it, would, one way or another, dramatically affect every member of his immediate family, from now and until the day they died.

What was his answer to be?

It was snowing! For the first time in ten years, declared the radio announcer, there would be snow on Christmas. The windshield wipers kept time with Bing Crosby, who comes back to life every December just to sing "White Christmas." The lump in his throat was almost more than he could handle. Would this be a Christmas "just like the ones I used to know"? Could she—*would* she—consider taking him back?

Although bone-weary from staying up all night and from the frantic search for airline reservations, he was far too tense to be sleepy. The flight had been a noisy one, and a colicky baby right behind him had ensured a wide-awake trip. He'd rented a car, and now . . . his heart pounded louder as each mile slipped past on the odometer.

Now that he had thrown away the most precious things in life—his wife and child—he no longer even had a home. Belatedly, he realized that without that, life's skies for him would lose their blue. How odd that his mind meshed the graying of his personal skies with the cold-graying of Cathy's eyes when he mentioned divorce: the blue of both was now as silvery as the ice- and snow-bedecked trees that flashed by.

The road became icier and he narrowly averted an accident several times. Occasionally a vehicle would spin out of control in front of him, but somehow he got around them safely.

At last! The city limits. He could hardly keep his runaway heart from jumping its tracks.

Had the road to his house ever seemed so long? Then he turned that last corner . . . Darkness: no lights, no car! He fought panic as he skidded into the driveway, got out, and fought the bitterly cold wind and snow to the back door. Inside, all appeared normal—nothing to indicate that Cathy and Julie had left on a long trip.

Maybe they were at his parents' house! He rushed back to the car, backed out onto the street, and sped out of town, hoping against hope that he was guessing right. He didn't dare to trust his fate to a telephone call.

About an hour later he saw the cheery lights of his folks' place. Through the front window he could see the multicolored lights on the Christmas tree. And *there,* in the driveway, was his wife's car.

He passed the house, then circled back on an alley road, cutting his lights as he reapproached the house. His heart now thumping like a jackhammer, he brushed off his clothes and shoes and ever so quietly opened the back door and stepped into the gloom of the dark hall.

He heard a child's voice, singing. He edged around the corner into the foyer. Kerosene lamps, as always, gave to the room a dreamy serenity. His folks sat on the couch intensely watching their grandchild as she softly sang, kneeling by his nativity stable:

> Silent night, holy night,
> All is calm, all is bright . . .

There was a look of ethereal beauty about her, lost as she was in her Bethlehem world.

"Oh, God," he prayed, "shield her from trouble, from pain—from growing up too soon."

Then, like a sword thrust through his chest, came the realization that he—her own father—had thrust her out of that protected world that children need so desperately if they are to retain their illusions, that childlike trust without which none of us will ever reach heaven's gate.

The sweet but slightly wobbly voice continued, then died away with the almost whispered

> Jesus, Lord, at Thy birth,
> Jesus, Lord, at Thy birth.

271

His heart wrenched as he drank in every inch of that frail flowering of the love he and Cathy had planted. Oh, how little it would take to blight that fragile blossom!

He wondered what his daughter had been told. . . . Would she still love him? Would she ever again trust him completely?

Upon completion of the beloved Austrian hymn, Julie sank down to the level of the nativity figures and, propping her head on her elbows, gazed fixedly into another time.

John now turned to an older version of Julie; this one leaned against the window frame. She was wearing a rose-colored gown that, in the flickering light from the oak logs in the fireplace, revealed rare beauty of face and form. But her face—such total desolation John had never seen before. In all the years that followed, that image of suffering was so indelibly burned into his memory that he was never able to bury it in his subconscious.

How woebegone, how utterly weary, she appeared. A lone tear glistened as it trickled down that cheek he had loved to kiss.

Oh, how he loved her!

He could hold back no longer. Silently, he approached her. Was it too late?

Suddenly, she sensed his presence and turned away from the vista of falling snow to look at him. She delayed the moment of reckoning by initially refusing to meet his eyes . . . then, very slowly, she raised her wounded eyes to his . . . and searched for an answer.

Oh, the relief that flooded over him when he saw her eyes widen as they were engulfed by the tidal wave of love that thundered across the five-foot abyss between them. In fact, it was so overwhelming that neither could ever remember how the distance was bridged—only that, through his tears, he kept saying, as he crushed her to him, "Oh, Cathy! Oh, Cathy! Forgive me, Cathy. Oh, Cathy, I love you so!"

And then there were three at the window—not counting the snow-coated teddy bear—the rest of the world forgotten in the regained heaven of their own.

And the snow of Christmas Eve continued to fall.

A NOTE FROM THE EDITORS

This book was selected by the Book and Inspirational Media Division of the company that publishes *Guideposts*, a monthly magazine filled with true stories of hope and inspiration.

Guideposts is available by subscription. All you have to do is write to Guideposts, 39 Seminary Hill Road, Carmel, New York 10512. When you subscribe, each month you can count on receiving exciting new evidence of God's presence, His guidance and His limitless love for all of us.

Guideposts Books are available on the World Wide Web at www.guidepostsbooks.com. Follow our popular book of devotionals, *Daily Guideposts*, and read excerpts from some of our best-selling books. You can also send prayer requests to our Monday morning Prayer Fellowship and read stories from recent issues of our magazines, *Guideposts, Angels on Earth*, and *Guideposts for Teens*.

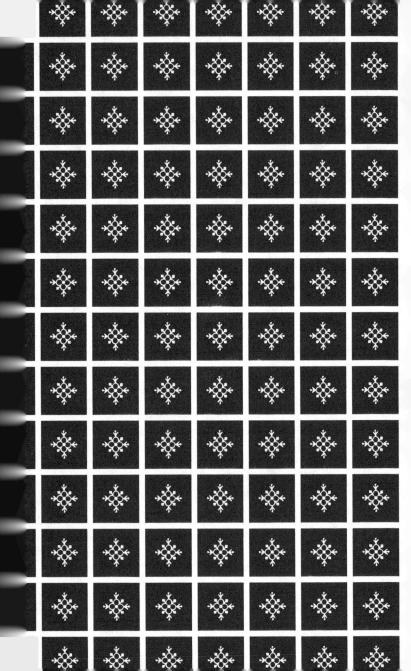